Advance Praise for Richie Norton and
The Power of Starting Something Stupid

"Perfect book for these uncertain times."

—**STEVE FORBES**, Chairman and Editor-in-Chief of
Forbes Media

"Richie Norton has written a book about courage. The
courage to do work that matters and to do it with your
heart and your soul. Go make something happen."

—**SETH GODIN**, author of *The Icarus Deception*

"Once in a great while a new author bursts on the scene
to light a fire under us. Richie Norton is that rare spark.
His certainty that the secret to success is to *start something stupid* is right on and will alter your future. Thirty
publishers thought Chicken Soup was stupid before it
sold over 100 million copies. This new book could not
have come at a better time and Richie's urgent and
authentic style is readable, convincing and a compelling blueprint for success. Be smart: read *The Power of
Starting Something Stupid*."

—**JACK CANFIELD**, *New York Times* bestselling author of
The Success Principles, and cocreator of the Chicken
Soup for the Soul® series

"I absolutely *love* this book. I love how it makes me feel.
It energizes me, inspires me, and gives me confidence.
It reminds each of us that all things are possible. . . .

This book disrupts conventional thinking—in a smart way."

—**STEPHEN M. R. COVEY**, *New York Times* and the #1 *Wall Street Journal* bestselling author of *The Speed of Trust* and coauthor of the #1 Amazon bestseller *Smart Trust*

"When I wrote *The E-Myth Revisited,* I wasn't an author and I really wasn't interested in business, but I had discovered something about business that nobody else seemed to see, or understand, and I decided to write a book about it. It came like a gift, a huge aha from out of nowhere, and I ran with it. Today, that 'stupid' idea (everybody told me it wouldn't work!) has created the most successful book on small business ever written because of that one, great stupid idea. I thought I was just lucky. Richie just told me that I'm in really good company. Find out why stupid is now the New Smart. Read it, you'll love it, you'll find out why thinking stupid makes the best sense in the world."

—**MICHAEL GERBER**, the world's #1 small-business guru and author of the bestselling *The E-Myth Revisited*

"More than just a call to action. This book is a demand for it. One chapter in I felt an involuntary impulse to reexamine my life. Later chapters held my hand as inevitable considerations came up from that process. An important, compelling and authentic read."

—**JOSEPH GRENNY**, *New York Times* bestselling coauthor of *Crucial Conversations* and *Change Anything*

"This warm, wonderful book will inspire and motivate you to do more in your life than you ever dreamed possible."
—**BRIAN TRACY**, author of *The Power of Self-Confidence*

"Sometimes a book shines a light on a topic in such a unique way that you find yourself slapping your forehead and saying to yourself, 'Now that's simply brilliant! Why have I never thought of it that way before?' And then you keep reading, and discover more and more 'stupidly brilliant' insights. This book makes you look forward to starting something stupid. That's the genius of it. If success in life is a goal of yours, you'd be smart to read this book ASAP."
—**ROBERT G. ALLEN**, author of the *New York Times* bestsellers *Nothing Down, Creating Wealth, Multiple Streams of Income,* and *The One Minute Millionaire*

"*The Power of Starting Something Stupid* teaches one of the truths that I have found in life and business: whenever I think something is a totally genius idea, it is not, and when I take a chance to do something that may seem like it will turn into nothing, that's when things turn out to be successful. So many great, successful ideas started as a whim—as something stupid. Because of this, I just keep trying. I just keep putting things out there. I just keep taking chances, even though they scare me."
—**GINA BIANCHINI**, CEO of Mightybell.com; cofounder of Ning.com

"Richie Norton has taken the fundamental principles of learning, living and thriving and integrated them in a most engaging and practical manner. His message and its relevance to every entrepreneur will be immediately apparent, but it is equally valuable and valid whatever endeavors and dreams you may have and at whatever age you find yourself. As he so compellingly explains, each of us can have a more engaging, rewarding and fulfilling life by applying these principles in pursuit of our most worthy goals. I would recommend this book to young and old alike who want to have each day be an exciting and rewarding adventure."

— DR. STEVEN C. WHEELWRIGHT, president of Brigham Young University–Hawaii; Edsel Bryant Ford Professor of Business Administration, Emeritus at Harvard Business School

"Richie Norton uncovers the paradox of stupid as the New Smart and shows us how success can be one idea away. Watch out: the energy in *The Power of Starting Something Stupid* is contagious. You may just find yourself starting something stupid and living your dreams."

— ANDY ANDREWS, *New York Times* bestselling author of *How Do You Kill 11 Million People?*, *The Noticer*, and *The Traveler's Gift*

"From the very first chapter, *The Power of Starting Something Stupid* opens your mind to the possibility that you're not living up to your full potential. Richie

Norton's powerful words provide the motivation and energy you'll need to start something stupid. Something amazingly, courageously, stupid!"

—**ANDY BEAL**, coauthor of *Radically Transparent*, CEO of Trackur.com

"In this era of negativity, less, limitations, and no, *The Power of Starting Something Stupid* offers hope, inspiration, and profound advice for moving toward our own positive futures. Richie Norton has tapped into what is good, positive, and worthwhile in all of us. Richie's perspective should be read and understood by all."

—**MARY TEAGARDEN**, professor of global strategy and editor, Thunderbird International Business Review at Thunderbird School of Global Management

"There's magic to this book: ideas which seem to be stupid often turn out to be brilliant—they only looked stupid because we hadn't seen them before, and it took courage for their creators to stick to their visions and bring them to light. Learning to curate, cultivate, and play with ideas that others don't understand (or are openly critical of!) is a hallmark of great innovators. Richie helps us to realize that fear of looking stupid can stop us from participating fully in life and from finding significant ways to help others. By showing us how this 'stupid to brilliant' pattern is at the heart of continuous innovation and renewal, he encourages us to trust ourselves and to bring our own unique contributions to our homes, our communities, our workplaces, and the world."

—**STEVE HARGADON**, founder of Classroom 2.0 and
Future of Education

"F. Scott Fitzgerald wrote, 'The test of a first-rate intelligence is the ability to hold two opposing ideas in mind at the same time and still retain the ability to function,' and understanding the New Smart is starting something stupid. When people like Fred Smith (FedEx), John Bogle (Vanguard), and Richard Branson (Virgin) created businesses that went in the opposite direction of the marketplace, they were once called stupid. All of these people transformed their industries and rose to the top as they focused on seeking the less obvious and taking the road less traveled. Richie takes readers on a journey to explore why starting something stupid may be the smartest thing you can do."

—**AARON BARE**, Entrepreneur-in-Residence, Thunderbird
Global School of Management; Former CEO and
Chairman, National Association of Sales Professionals

"Today I have over 120 million YouTube views; it only seems like yesterday when people thought that following my dreams could only be a hobby. Fortunately, as Richie teaches, 'stupid' was the smartest thing I could do."

—**DEVIN GRAHAM**, content creator for the YouTube
channel devinsupertramp

THE POWER OF
STARTING SOMETHING
STUPID

THE POWER OF
STARTING SOMETHING
STUPID

HOW TO CRUSH FEAR,
MAKE DREAMS HAPPEN, AND
LIVE WITHOUT REGRET

RICHIE NORTON

with **NATALIE NORTON**

SHADOW
MOUNTAIN

For my brilliant, generous and beautiful wife, Natalie.

And for my sons Raleigh, Cardon, Lincoln, and Gavin.
May this book inspire you to go and do something totally amazing.

—RICHIE NORTON

For my brother, Gavin.

—NATALIE NORTON

Interior illustrations by Barry Hansen

© 2013 Richie Norton

All rights reserved. No part of this book may be reproduced in any form or by any means without permission in writing from the publisher, Shadow Mountain®. The views expressed herein are the responsibility of the author and do not necessarily represent the position of Shadow Mountain.

Visit us at ShadowMountain.com

Library of Congress Cataloging-in-Publication Data
Norton, Richie, author.
   The power of starting something stupid / Richie Norton with Natalie Norton.
      pages cm
   Includes bibliographical references and index.
   ISBN 978-1-60907-009-0 (hardbound : alk. paper) 1. Success in business. 2. Creative ability in business. I. Title.
   HF5386.N596 2013
   650.1—dc23   2012023695

Printed in the United States of America
Edwards Brothers Malloy, Ann Arbor, MI

10 9 8 7 6 5 4 3 2

Contents

Foreword

by Stephen M. R. Covey

One of the great lessons I remember my dad constantly emphasizing in our family while I was growing up was "Use your R&I." That is, use your resourcefulness and initiative. He taught us that we were not victims of the circumstances surrounding us, but rather masters of our own destiny. This mindset became the powerful beginning habit of *The 7 Habits of Highly Effective People*—"Be Proactive." *The Power of Starting Something Stupid* beautifully captures the spirit of that energizing principle. We are not merely scripted by our circumstances; we can become the creative forces of our lives, capable of optimizing sometimes even unseen possibilities.

I absolutely *love* this book. I love how it makes me feel. It energizes me, inspires me, and gives me confidence. It reminds each of us that all things are possible, that life is short, and to take action now. Simultaneously, Richie Norton rightly cautions us that our actions must be tempered by our integrity to our values, and that in

order to harness the full power of our personal authenticity, we must first check our motives. He teaches that our
motives should be driven by our intent to benefit others.

That is why I so resonate with Richie. From the first
time I heard him speak, I sensed his sincere and passionate desire to bless others. I've watched him rise to
life's challenges and develop both the character and the
competency necessary to earn the credibility needed to
significantly influence others in meaningful ways. He
has become a bold and courageous leader—and I believe
you'll see that through his work.

You likely picked up this book because you are seeking encouragement to seize life's challenges and more
courageously chase your dreams. Perhaps a trusted
friend recommended this book to you. Perhaps you were
simply intrigued by the title. However you found this
book, I encourage you to read it immediately. There is
no perfect time to start the next level of your life. This
inspiring book will teach you—whether you're starting
your career, in mid-career, or ending your career—that
the smartest thing you can do is to live life as if your best
days are always ahead of you and then act on your inspiration—to start something "stupid."

There are many reasons why I like this book but let
me highlight three:

First, this book disrupts conventional thinking—in

a smart way. It's fresh, relevant, and cuts through the noise of detractors and competing voices. The world-stage is changing around us like waves in the ocean at an unprecedented speed. To aid you in navigating the changing seas of life, *The Power of Starting Something Stupid* stands as a beacon of light that helps bring clarity, focus, and drive to your everyday life with a paradoxical combination of unconventional yet timeless principles that bring lasting success. This book teaches you how to identify what is most important to you, innovate incrementally, and overcome fear, pride, and procrastination so you can reach your highest aspirations.

Second, it's no surprise that I particularly liked the principles of service and trust in the section called START—a term Richie coined—that identifies how successful people Serve, Thank, Ask, Receive, and Trust. These principles, when put into practice upon initiating a "stupid idea," are imperative to all people and organizations that want to inspire a revolution of creativity, innovation, and influence. START is a brilliant and effective principle-centered approach to help jump-start any project, increase engagement, and reach big-picture goals.

Third, Richie Norton is that rare individual who successfully combines both character and competence, courage and consideration, humility and professional will. The net result is that Richie gives his readers an author they can trust.

The Power of Starting Something Stupid has made me reflect back on my own life and work. In doing so, it dawned on me that my most meaningful success, in both my business and personal life, started with something stupid. As the book teaches, "Stupid is the New Smart," and the "New Smart" decisions I made were defining moments in my life.

This book has rekindled my spirit and given me a renewed outlook on life and business—and I'm confident it will do the same for you.

As Richie says, "Life's too short not to start something stupid." I'm already getting started on my next stupid idea. Read and apply this book and make your own stupid idea your New Smart reality.

STEPHEN M. R. COVEY
New York Times and the #1 *Wall Street Journal* bestselling author of *The Speed of Trust* and coauthor of the #1 Amazon bestseller *Smart Trust*

THE POWER OF
STARTING SOMETHING
STUPID

PART
I

Stupid Is the New Smart

"Stay hungry. Stay foolish."—STEVE JOBS

"The difference between genius and stupidity is: genius has its limits."—ALBERT EINSTEIN

"First he told me it was a stupid idea . . . and then he agreed to come on board."—PIERRE OMIDYAR, FOUNDER OF EBAY

"A lot of people thought it sounded stupid. . . . Even some of our engineers weren't interested."
—BIZ STONE, COFOUNDER OF TWITTER

"Everything I do people think is stupid."—SETH GODIN, BESTSELLING AUTHOR

"We don't like their sound, and guitar music is on the way out."—DECCA RECORDING CO., REJECTING THE BEATLES, 1962

"'Are you crazy? Stick my face on the label of salad dressing?'"—Paul Newman, founder of Newman's Own

"When I proposed that idea people laughed at me, saying no one would go to the airport without a paper ticket. . . . Now everyone does, and it has saved the industry millions of dollars."—David Neeleman, CEO of JetBlue Airways, on the advent of the electronic airline ticket

"We allow no geniuses around our Studio."
—Walt Disney

"The fool doth think he is wise, but the wise man knows himself to be a fool."—William Shakespeare

"Here's to the crazy ones. The rebels. The trouble-makers. The ones who see things differently. While some may see them as the crazy ones, we see genius. Because the people who are crazy enough to think they can change the world, are the ones who do."—Apple, Inc.

Behind great success lies a common denominator: stupid.

After conducting hundreds of personal interviews, drawing from academic cases, and building on extensive study of famous and everyday people alike, a surprising trend emerged. Successful people, throughout history and today, don't avoid stupid, *they lean into it* . . . in a smart way.

LIVE TO START ↰
↳ START TO LIVE

1

What You Must Know First: Gavin's Law

A decision had to be made. The impossible decision.
A nurse quietly entered the room and injected a dose of epinephrine into his I.V. I wouldn't have noticed her, except that when she left, she slid the glass door closed behind her and drew the outer curtain for our privacy.

We were alone. After days and days of incessant attention by multiple doctors and hospital staff, the room was completely quiet. Quiet, that is, aside from the gentle rise and fall of the ventilator and the soft *beep, beep, beep* of the heart monitor.

Adrenaline coursed madly through my veins. The room spun around me as I sat, disoriented to the point of nausea, on a stool beside his bed. I gripped the bed rail to keep from tipping over. But I wasn't watching him. My eyes were glued to her as she fell into the chair in the corner of the room and wept, chest heaving, face pressed hard into her hands.

"This is a decision we shouldn't have to make," she said almost imperceptibly, as she ran her hands frantically through her hair, pulling it tight away from her face.

Agony. There wasn't any other word. I took her hands in mine and looked deeply into her eyes, and together, we made the impossible decision: Do not resuscitate.

Those were the wee hours of the morning on January 7, 2010.

Two Years Earlier

On a sunny Hawaiian day, in the spring of 2007, Gavin took a gray, plastic container and placed his journals, a beat-up card containing the prayer of St. Francis of Assisi, and a few other precious possessions inside. He sealed the box and labeled it "To be opened 2027." He took a Sharpie and adorned his treasure chest with a clever little drawing of a pirate and a short note to himself that read, "Hello, old man Gavin!"

He got on his salt-rusted beach cruiser, carefully balanced the box on his lap and pedaled with bare feet toward the lush Hawaiian mountains. Gavin had called Hawaii home for more than five years—nearly a quarter of his young life—and he wanted to leave a piece of his heart with the island that had taught and given him so much. He buried his treasure at the base of the beautiful Ko'olauloa Mountains, intending not to open it again for twenty years.

It was only a few short weeks later, however, that those journals were unearthed, and I found myself reading excerpts from them to a grief-stricken audience of hundreds who had gathered to celebrate his incredible young life. Less than three weeks after burying his time capsule, my healthy and vibrant young brother-in-law passed away unexpectedly in his sleep.

He was twenty-one years old.

A little over two years after Gavin's death, my wife, Natalie, gave birth to our fourth son. With pride, we named our little guy after his late uncle. Baby Gavin was born October 24, 2009. He was perfect, and even his rough-and-tumble big brothers agreed.

Yet here we sat, only ten short weeks into his life, alone in a hospital room. Alone except for the quiet nurse and her epinephrine. Natalie on one side of Gavin, and I on the other, the words "Do not resuscitate" ringing heavily in our ears as tears stung the edges of our raw eyes.

My initial response had been to give our son every fighting chance at survival. *"Of course we will resuscitate!"* I had confidently said. I was baffled that the doctors even had the audacity to ask. Words and phrases began pounding through my brain, clouding my thinking, impairing my sense of reason, and damming my judgment completely: "pertussis," "secondary infection," "experimental procedure," "end of the line," "nothing more we can do," "time to say good-bye." Then slowly, very slowly, the reality of our situation started to set in. I finally came to see the absolute hopelessness we were facing. I became aware that the violent process of resuscitation in and of itself would only lengthen Gavin's suffering and not save his life. I swallowed, hard. And I gathered the courage to let go.

Natalie and I cried together. We spoke words of deep, profound love to our sweet little son. And moments later, my sweet wife rocked him tenderly in her arms, and I rested my hand on our son's chest and felt the last beats of his tiny heart. We sang him a lullaby through our tears, and our boy was gone.

The weight of the world never felt heavier in my hands than it did the day we walked out of that hospital with empty arms.

Baby Gavin lived seventy-six days.

> *"Don't be fooled by the calendar. There are only as many days . . . as you make use of."*
> —CHARLES RICHARDS, CANADIAN JUDGE

Gavin's Law

Very shortly after the death of our son, my wife, Natalie, and I went to listen to a friend and mentor of mine who was giving a speech at a university near our home in Hawaii. After her presentation, she came to where we were sitting to say hello and to offer her condolences. After chatting for a few moments, she looked Natalie straight in the eye, and abruptly asked, "So, what have you learned?" Admittedly, I was somewhat taken aback by the intensity of her question. Thankfully, Natalie— always on her toes—offered a gracious, eloquent, and genuine response, as I stood by, somewhat dumb-founded.

The months passed, but I couldn't forget this question:

"So, what have you learned?"

That question changed my life. Here were the facts: my brother-in-law was gone, our son was gone, and there wasn't a thing in the world I could do to change any of that. Suddenly, my life took on a very real sense of urgency. There was, in fact, a time limit!

Transcendent to the sense of urgency I felt, I found myself face to face with the realization that circumstance was completely outside my realm of control. Not only this particular set of circumstances, but circumstance in general. I suddenly realized that if we are sitting around

waiting—maybe even begging and pleading—for our circumstances to change so that we can finally live life the
way we really want to live, chances are very good that we
will stay stuck waiting *forever.*

There will always be a million reasons to wait until
later. This is simply the nature of the animal called *life.*
Those Gavins taught me to live, today. I've summed up
the lesson I learned from the deaths of my brother-in-law
and my son into what I call Gavin's Law:

Live to start. Start to live.

Don't Wait. Start Stuff.

People are innately passionate about certain unique aspects of life. *You* are innately passionate about certain
unique aspects of life. And people are blessed with bouts
of clear and concise intuition that drive them toward
distinct goals and aspirations within their jobs and their
lives as a whole. (*You* are not excluded from this group.)
But people disregard these inspired thoughts, these high-
potential opportunities, as "just another stupid idea."

Why?

Perhaps they are concerned about a lack of support
(perceived or otherwise) from others, or maybe they
are afraid of what others will think of them if they fail.
Whatever the reason, they convince themselves:

"This would be a great idea for someone who has more free time."

"This would be a great idea for someone with a higher level of education."

"This would be a great idea for someone who has more money."

"Everybody thinks this idea is crazy. They must be right."

No matter the justification, the response is the same. These inspired thoughts, these *high-potential* ideas, are stuffed deep into the drawer labeled "stupid," and they're never heard from again . . . or the waiting game begins.

People wait.

They wait for that elusive day when they'll finally have enough time (guess what?—you never will), enough education (there is always more to know), enough money (no matter how much you make, someone will always have more). They wait until the children are grown (news flash: just because they're grown, it doesn't mean you're rid of them) or until things settle down at work (they never will). People wait until . . . until . . . until . . . They wait, and they wait, and they wait, until that fateful day when they wake up and realize that while they were sitting around, paying dues, earning their keep, waiting for that elusive "perfect time," their entire life has passed them by.

Consciously living and breathing Gavin's Law in every facet of my life and business has helped me realize the importance, the satisfaction, and the very real *power* that comes from starting something stupid. If you let it, Gavin's Law will change your life, forever.

There is no greater time than *now* to start moving toward achieving your goals. *Don't wait. Start stuff.* Live to start your stupid ideas, and start to live a life without regret—a life filled with meaning, freedom, happiness, fun, authenticity, and influence. After all, now is, in all actuality, the only time you're truly guaranteed.

Life is too short not to start something stupid.

"Everything can be taken from a man but one thing: the last of the human freedoms—to choose one's attitude in any given set of circumstances, to choose one's own way."

—Viktor E. Frankl, author of *Man's Search for Meaning*

STUPID IS THE NEW SMART

2

The Anatomy of Stupid as the New Smart: Used Blue Jeans and the Creative Puzzle

"In every work of genius we recognize our own rejected thoughts; they come back to us with a certain alienated majesty."
—RALPH WALDO EMERSON

It was the mid-1980s. Clay Leavitt, a Canadian teaching English in Japan at the time, noticed something interesting that quickly had his undivided attention. Almost overnight, the teens he was teaching were showing up in class wearing faded Levis and other denim clothing. Clay recalls, "All of a sudden, youth worldwide were watching MTV and other programs and seeing the same fashion trends, especially the street-youth fashion of the United States. Overnight, or so it appeared, jean pants became an 'Americana' fashion craze."

The wheels in Clay's head started to turn. "My wife and I got curious, and we asked some of the kids where they shopped. When we visited the 'retro' shops that they told us about, we were amazed that they were selling

Levis and other brands of jeans and jackets for incredibly high prices." The same jeans and jackets that were readily available in US thrift stores (where they sold for only a dollar or two), were being sold in Japan for the equivalent of a hundred US dollars or more! There was even a collector's market where people would buy older pairs of used jeans and jackets for thousands of dollars! "I still own a jacket that at the time could have sold for over ten thousand dollars," Clay relates.

Upon moving from Japan to the United States, Clay had already determined that he would start his own company selling used jeans in Japan. He began to further research the market and found that there was demand for used jeans, not just in Japan, but in many parts of the world. In fact, Clay soon found that there were even buyers who would buy them "sight unseen for silly prices." Things looked promising, but there were bills to pay, and his wife was expecting their first son. So Clay got in touch with an old friend and college roommate, Dal Zemp, and hit him up for a job.

One day at work, Clay mentioned his crazy idea to Dal and another associate, John Pennington. He asked them if they were interested in helping him collect jeans in order to set up a side business selling specialty clothing overseas.

"Their reaction was similar to my family's," said Clay.

"'That sounds pretty crazy. Why would anyone want to buy someone else's used jeans, especially for the prices that you're saying they will pay?'" Clay explained as best he could, but both Dal and John were very skeptical. After all, these were some serious claims.

"The next morning, John came into the office with several pair of Levi 501s and wanted to know how much they were worth. I looked at them," Clay said, "and told him they were worth about eighty to a hundred dollars to the English buyer, maybe more if we could find someone in Japan that would buy them."

"'Wow!' John said, 'I found these in the garbage Dumpster behind my house.' We never decided if that was just the world's biggest coincidence, or whether it was God's hand in our lives, but that was the beginning of a great partnership that lasted for the next ten years."

"Those were exciting days: weekend drives to Boise, Phoenix, Denver, and anywhere else we could find thrift stores that would sell to us, and then back to Salt Lake with our cars stuffed so full of jeans that we were dragging bottom—all in time to be to work on Monday morning."

In the beginning, their main markets were Germany, Japan, France, England, and Italy, but they quickly expanded into some unlikely countries, such as Korea, Thailand, and others. They were doing trade shows in

Europe and tripping all over Asia and Europe, knocking on the doors of stores, small and large. Before they knew it, they were advertising on television, and even the national press picked up on their story. Soon they were inundated with calls and orders from buyers all over the world. In 1989, Clay and Dal moved their families to Europe in order to take advantage of higher pricing by being closer to the market. Clay recalls:

> Dal moved his family to Germany and rented a warehouse/store in a little town outside of Munich where he began to develop a network of smaller buyers, usually store owners. One day, he decided to try a local warehouse sale event. He advertised in the newspaper, but mostly with low-cost fliers handed out at the local schools to let students know they could buy direct from the warehouse. The next day there was a lineup of kids wanting to buy jeans. I think we sold $70,000 worth of jeans that weekend.

It wasn't all smooth sailing. There were many difficult decisions to be made, and there were difficult hurdles to be overcome. "There were detractors," recalls Clay. "Lots of people asked us if what we were doing was even legal. My mother asked me if I was sure that I wanted to throw away six years of business school, and my life, to sell used jeans. I'm sure she thought it was a phase and that it would pass." And, of course, people thought they were crazy, but of that Clay says, "Sure it sounded stupid. But we knew what we knew, and the money was real."

> **"Sure it sounded stupid. But we knew what we knew, and the money was real."**

The Paradox of Stupid as the New Smart

Let me whisper a secret directly into your ear: If someone thinks that your ideas, or the changes you want to make, or the dreams bubbling up inside of you, are stupid, welcome to the Club. You're in the company of the world's leading innovators, change agents, thought leaders, inventors, entrepreneurs, intrapreneurs, philanthropists, executives, employees, educators, youth, moms, dads, families, philosophers, mentors, and more.

We all want to be smart. We're scared of failure. Scared of falling behind. Scared of being foolish. Scared of looking stupid. No one wants any of that.

Or do we?

Maybe the smartest people in the world know something we don't. Maybe they know that in order to be smart, in order to make significant contributions to the world, and in order to spur significant change in their own lives, they sometimes have to act on ideas that others might initially perceive as stupid.

The traditional idea of stupidity is as old as time. Pick up any dictionary, and it will offer some derivative of the definition, "lacking intelligence and common sense." This type of stupidity is what I call *unhealthy stupid*. It is dangerous, and clearly not the kind of stupid you want to embrace. Unhealthy stupid indicates that a thing or idea is *inherently* faulty, meaning that the stupidity is a permanently ingrained and inseparable element.

Stupid as the New Smart, on the other hand, is healthy and should be sought after and embraced. Stupid as the New Smart is that pressing thought that just won't go away. That nagging hunch, that golden idea, that lofty dream, that if it weren't so seemingly "stupid," might actually have the chance to become something truly significant—in your own life, and quite possibly, *in the world at large.*

> *Stupid as the New Smart* infers that while an idea may *appear* to be inherently faulty, the idea is, in reality, sound and in your best interest to pursue.

The New Smart, is *not* inherently stupid. Rather, these ideas are simply labeled as such by yourself or others due to doubt, fear, confusion, or lack of understanding.

In short, stupid as the New Smart is a paradox.

> **par·a·dox / 'per-ə-ˌdäks/**
> Noun: a seemingly absurd or contradictory statement
> or proposition which when investigated may
> prove to be well founded or true.

For the sake of clarity, let's compare the phenomenon of stupid as the New Smart to what anthropologist Grant McCracken defines as "culturematic." After observing cultural innovations in contemporary culture, McCracken said, "a culturematic is a little machine for making culture. It is designed to do three things: test the world, discover meaning, and unleash value." In an interview with *Harvard Business Review,* McCracken further explained:

> The paradox we're running up against here, and the point of proceeding culturematically is precisely that some of the things [that] seemed least productive, or promising of value, are actually the things that are going to be most rewarding for us.
>
> [For example,] Fantasy Football, which was

created by three sports journalists in a Manhattan hotel room . . . is now an industry worth $3.5 billion. They created this idea [and] thought so little of it that they didn't take out trademarks, or copyrights, and patents. As a result of which, they did not participate in this creation of value. But there it was.

And you can just imagine. It's like Twitter in the early days. When people said, oh, this is stupid. Nobody's going to want to use this. In the case of Fantasy Football, people said, well, why would you want to have an alternative sports reality when you have the National Football League? Surely that's sufficient. Surely that's plenty.

> **The art of optimizing the New Smart**
> **is to identify and act on ideas that may**
> **appear to be of lesser value, but are,**
> **in actuality, most rewarding.**

Here are some ways the New Smart shows up in our lives:

- The New Smart is highly creative.
- The New Smart is counterintuitive.
- The New Smart is innovative.
- The New Smart is beyond our comfort zone.
- The New Smart is making change.

- The New Smart is unconventional.
- The New Smart is leaning into fear.
- The New Smart is pushing through less-than-ideal circumstances.
- The New Smart is turning down the volume on critics.
- The New Smart is trusting the voice inside your own head.

Paradoxically, stupid as the New Smart is the power behind the world's wave makers and mountain movers.

It's important to note that the New Smart isn't being flippant and making decisions without forethought or preparation. Those types of behaviors would be classified as unhealthy stupid. The New Smart is having the ability to discern when the label of "stupid" is masking a smart idea. Embracing the New Smart requires employing ample forethought and preparation, and then committing to move forward against the current of the discouraging and even condemning opinions of others.

The Stupid Filter: Unlimited Opportunity

When you begin to look at the world through the *stupid filter,* you'll see successful, stupid ideas everywhere you look. Doggles (yes, fashion sunglasses for dogs) pulls in an estimated $3 million a year; approximately half a million Chia Pets are sold each holiday season; and Angry Birds creator, Rovio, confirmed a profit of $106 million in 2011. (Yes, $106 million from a game where players do nothing more than fling birds at pigs.) Seeing "stupid" as opportunity can be very profitable.

Sara Blakely, founder of Spanx, saw opportunity in starting something others thought was stupid—*form-fitting, footless pantyhose*. She became the youngest self-made female billionaire, turning $5,000 of personal savings into $1 billion with her crazy idea to revolutionize hosiery. She said, "[I] approached several lawyers who thought my idea was so crazy that they later admitted thinking I had been sent by Candid Camera." When she approached hosiery manufacturers "they all thought the idea was stupid or didn't make sense." However, Blakely leaned into the New Smart—just because someone else thought the idea was "stupid" and "wouldn't sell" didn't mean it was true.

Blakely's persistence paid off. She says, "I received a call from a mill owner who said he 'decided to help make my crazy idea.' When asked why he had the change of heart, he said, 'I have two daughters.' Turns out they didn't think the idea was crazy at all." Just like that, the mill owner had a paradigm shift: what once was stupid became the New Smart.

It's not just in niche spaces, nor is it merely among

the blatantly stupid, that we notice a trend of stupid success. It's *everywhere*. The New Smart is found from the cars that you drive to the celebrities you endorse to the computers you can't live without. It's in your favorite fashion trends, the type of music you listen to, and the innovative ideas in the books that you read. The New Smart can be found in the small, everyday choices you make as well as your biggest, most potentially life-altering decisions.

Just a Stupid Idea?

New Smart ideas and individuals have literally changed the world. Consider this quick handful of examples:

The telephone. Western Union originally rejected the telephone, saying in an internal memo in 1876, "The device is inherently of no value to us."

The automobile. In 1903, the president of Michigan Savings Bank advised Henry Ford's lawyer not to invest in the Ford Motor Company. "The horse is here to stay but the automobile is only a novelty, a fad."

The radio. In response to David's Sarnoff's urgings for investment in the radio in the 1920s, his associates said, "The wireless music box has no imaginable commercial value. Who would pay for a message sent to nobody in particular?"

Man on the Moon. In 1957, Lee De Forest, the

man who pioneered radio and invented the vacuum tube, said, "A man-made moon voyage will never occur regardless of all future scientific advances."

Satellites. In 1961, T. Craven, the FCC commissioner said, "There is practically no chance communications space satellites will be used to provide better telephone, telegraph, television, or radio service inside the United States."

Thomas Edison. Said Edison himself, "I don't know now what it was, but I was always at the foot of the class. I used to feel that the teachers never sympathized with me and that my father thought that I was stupid, and at last I almost decided that I must really be a dunce. . . . One day I overheard the teacher tell the inspector that I was 'addled' and it would not be worthwhile keeping me in school any longer."

Walt Disney. Walt Disney was fired by a newspaper editor because "he lacked imagination and had no good ideas."

Elvis Presley. Elvis, the king of rock and roll, was fired from the Grand Ole Opry after only one performance. "You ain't goin' nowhere, son. You ought to go back to drivin' a truck."

The list could go on for days.

These innovations and individuals spurred huge changes in the economy, the way we live, and the way we view the world. The New Smart has served as a catalyst that opened entirely new industries, creating hundreds of thousands of jobs in the process. People who lean into the New Smart courageously put on the metaphorical dunce cap and change the world.

> *"Whenever you see a successful business, someone once made a courageous decision."*
> —PETER DRUCKER, LEGENDARY MANAGEMENT CONSULTANT AND BUSINESS AUTHOR

When you look at life through the stupid filter, you quickly find that quite often the stuff that sticks is the selfsame stuff that someone, somewhere, once wrote off as "stupid." And if some of the world's greatest success stories weren't willing to stop at stupid, neither should you.

Innate Sensibility

While the process of differentiation between unhealthy stupid and the New Smart requires significant fore-thought, assessment, and research, another critical component to this process of differentiation, far too often overlooked, is an authentic trust in your inherent sense of direction.

This inherent sense of direction is what I call your *innate sensibility,* and it's about as easy to explain as nailing a wave upon the shore. Bestselling author and former CEO of General Electric, Jack Welch, once described *trust* by saying, "I could give you a dictionary definition, but you know it when you feel it." Drawing from this definition of trust, your innate sensibility is something you'll know when you feel it.

By its very nature, the New Smart is highly counterintuitive and will almost always go against the grain of conventional thinking, on a small or grand scale, but you can't afford to use that as an excuse to keep yourself stuck. Turn down the volume on detractors, and tune in to your own innate sensibility.

The Creative Puzzle: Innate Sensibility versus Enthusiasm

Imagine, if you will, that you're putting together a jigsaw puzzle. You dump out all the pieces, and then you begin the painstaking task of trying to make them all fit. Things start out fairly easily as you find the border pieces, and without much difficulty, you start to achieve some measure of structure. You begin to feel somewhat oriented. Then you start in on the body of the puzzle. Some areas come together effortlessly, others make you want to bang your head against the wall, but you stick with it, because you *know* that right in front of you is every single piece you need to complete this puzzle!

Actively pursuing stupid as the New Smart is the process of putting together what I call the *creative puzzle*—it's your responsibility to put the pieces together to make your idea a reality. The initial energy or enthusiasm surrounding an idea is clearly important and is akin to getting the edges placed in your jigsaw puzzle. But when detractors' voices (real or perceived, well-meaning or antagonistic) ring loud in your ears, poking holes in what, only moments before, felt solid and sure, it's your innate sensibility that will serve as the anchor to sustain you. This true sense of direction-filled conviction is the internal certainty that all the pieces are before you, and you just have to figure out how to make them all fit.

Innate sensibility fuels one's ability to cut directly through external complexity to a place of deeply seated conviction, wisdom, and direction. Adversely, enthusiasm denotes eagerness and excitement, but offers only a superficial sense of surety. Enthusiasm is important and can accelerate the growth of any idea exponentially; however, it is by nature shallow and emotionally based. All the enthusiasm in the world won't be enough to save you if you've run right down the rabbit hole called unhealthy stupid.

Ultimately, your idea must be anchored by a deep feeling of conviction in order for you to have the longevity (and the blood and guts) required to follow it through to completion.

Begin Anywhere, Begin Today

The lifeblood of any idea is provided completely by the willingness to *start*. Remember Gavin's Law: *Live to start. Start to live.* Individuals and organizations that live to start dreams, really do start living and breathing those dreams. It is distinctly significant that the title of this book is *The Power of Starting Something Stupid* rather than simply "The Power of Stupid" (an option I briefly entertained). The most challenging part of nearly any project is the initial exertion of energy (and courage) required to begin. Once you've overcome the often-debilitating power of resistance, the momentum to keep going leads from one thing to another until you reach your goals . . . or something even better.

The "Miracle of the Used Jeans" offers a perfect illustration of the very real power of starting. Here are the parting words from my interview with Clay:

> While part of any success is being in the right place at the right time, there is much of our success that we control by our decisions and actions. How many people, for example, saw the youth buying jeans for hundreds of dollars in Japan, were amazed, talked about it, but didn't do anything about it? We

went home and took action. Again and again, we made bold decisions without any hesitation.

When I look back, I'm amazed at some of the things that we "just did." We quit our jobs, moved our families around the world, traveled to some amazing places, organized sales all over Europe without even being able to speak the languages. But the important thing is that we did them. When we were faced with decisions, we made the best decision possible based on the information that we had available to us and then moved forward.

How many ideas, opportunities, businesses, and *lives* are squandered because we mistakenly suppress those so-called "stupid ideas." We all want to make the best decisions in life possible. Don't allow life to pass you by because you are afraid of stupid.

Opportunities will come and go, but if you do nothing about them, so will you.

DESTROY THE WAITING PLACE

3

Where You Don't Want to Be: Lost in Waiting

*"I plead with you not to let those most important things
pass you by as you plan for that illusive and nonexistent future
when you will have time to do all that you want to do.
Instead, find joy in the journey—now."*
—Thomas S. Monson, religious leader and author

I was twenty-four years old, newly married, just finishing college and poorer than dirt. I went to pitch one of my own stupid ideas to an investment banker—a multi-millionaire who had achieved success many times over.

He listened intently as I went over my business plan, then he leaned back in his chair and told me that I reminded him a lot of himself back when he was in college. Lost in nostalgia, he talked about how exciting and satisfying life had been in those days. Like me, he'd been active, happy, enthusiastic, and full of hope. Back then, he was living the lifestyle of his dreams.

He slowly shook his head, and with definite regret in his voice, told me that he had been working his entire adult life, all with the intent of *someday* getting back to the life he used to have when he was my age—the life my penniless, twenty-four-year-old self was living *right then*.

Before me sat a man who had pushed the pause button on his life. He had put his happiness and his dreams on hold for *decades* so that one elusive day, after he'd "paid his dues" and "earned his keep," he could finally live his dreams and be where he had always *really* wanted to be.

Now, here he sat, a lifetime later, still waiting to start living.

> *"How much of human life is lost in waiting!"*
> —RALPH WALDO EMERSON

Before my experience with the successful investment banker, I had always aimed to be successful, earn a respectable living, and make my mark on the world. (I still do.) But as I looked at the years of regret etched into that man's face, I thought, *Is this what I'm after? Is this the success I am seeking?* I knew that I would end up living a life of regret if I too got lost in the busyness of life—lost in waiting.

Then and there I made a decision: I refuse to achieve "success" at the expense of my life. The two—life success and genuine fulfillment—will have to go hand in hand, because I will not keep my head down for the next forty years only to look up at the end and say, "Now I can finally start living!"

The Activity Trap

Randy Komisar, a successful entrepreneur, a founding member of TiVo, and a partner at the venture capital firm Kleiner Perkins Caufield & Byers wrote an intriguing book entitled *The Monk and the Riddle: The Education of a Silicon Valley Entrepreneur.* In his book, Komisar discusses what he calls the "Deferred Life Plan." He explains that if you buy into this Deferred Life Plan school of thought, you are essentially opting to divide your life into two parts, or rather, two steps. "Step one: Do what you have to do. Then, eventually—Step two: Do what you want to do." There is a very real risk associated with this type of thinking.

Komisar says that people think "getting rich fast provides the quickest way to get past the first step." In other words, the faster you can fill your pockets (by doing what you have to do), the faster you can move on to step two, where you're finally able to "do what you want to do." That sounds about right.

Or does it?

> "For a long time it had seemed to me that life
> was about to begin—real life. But there was

*always some obstacle in the way, something to
be gotten through first, some unfinished business, time still to be served, a debt to be paid.
Then life would begin. At last it dawned on
me that these obstacles were my life."*
—ALFRED D'SOUZA, AUSTRALIAN WRITER
   AND PHILOSOPHER

There is a dangerous flaw in the Deferred Life Plan,
and it is outlined in one of my favorite analogies from Dr.
Stephen R. Covey. He said, "It's incredibly easy to get
caught up in an activity trap, in the busy-ness of life, to
work harder and harder at climbing the ladder of success
only to discover it's leaning against the wrong wall." The
lesson here is clear: make certain you've got your ladder leaning up against the right wall—that you are consciously aware of where you're headed—*before* you start
the climb. (Or, as Covey so concisely put it, "Begin with
the end in mind.")

*"When it's time to die, let us not discover that
we have never lived."*
—HENRY DAVID THOREAU

The very real danger inherent to the Deferred Life
Plan is that, according to Komisar, "The vast majority of
people will not become rich . . . and the lucky winners
may get to step two only to find themselves aimless, di-
rectionless." The poor souls who buy into the idea of the

Deferred Life Plan are bound to get caught in an activity trap—*constantly doing, but never achieving*. These individuals are so determined to get to step two ("do what you want to do") as quickly as humanly possible that they never take the time to stop and ensure that their ladder is leaning against the right wall.

The pursuit of prosperity shouldn't stop you from the pursuit of happiness.

Retirement Confusion and Planned Procrastination

As president of a financial services company, I spent several years working in the world of tax-deferred retirement consulting. I met with hundreds of individuals and couples, many in the golden years of life. As the years rolled by, these individuals began to realize that they'd deferred more than their taxes; they'd deferred their lives.

Many of my clients had tragically given in to the notion that waiting was the wisest course of action: "*When* I have more money I'll finally _____" or "*When* I retire I'll be able to _____." The common conversation in these meetings was, "When I'm sixty-five—but hopefully sooner—I will be able to relax, travel, donate to charity, spend time with my family, and give my time to the causes I care about. I will finally live the dreams I've waited for and worked my whole life to live."

> **Retirement confusion:** When people confuse the importance of saving money with the need to postpone pursuing dreams.

Many of the people I interviewed followed a life-plan that went something like this:

> Be a kid.
> Have dreams.
> Grow up.
> Finish school.
> Go to work.
> Make millions.
> Retire.
> Live dreams.

They prepared. They worked hard. They invested time and resources. Then they waited, for years, only to discover that life at the end of the retirement rainbow wasn't exactly what they thought it would be. Sometimes a spouse had passed away. Sometimes their health had declined. The stock market had taken an unexpected downturn, and many of them didn't have the money they'd expected to have (and on and on and on).

These wonderful, conscientious, patient, dedicated individuals had invested all their time, effort, and/or savings into a sinking ship, and now their treasure lay irretrievable upon the ocean floor. The tragedy isn't merely the treasure lost; it's the forty years of dreams postponed. Forty years of waiting—and those days are gone forever.

The concept of retirement planning is a good thing that has simply gone too far. Sadly, retirement planning, in many circumstances, has become nothing more than planned procrastination.

A Bit of History and Latest Trends

In the late 1800s, organizations in countries such as Germany and the United States began to offer pensions to meet the needs of the people. Often they put a restriction on the disbursement of retirement benefits and granted them only to the people who met the company's or the government's special requirements (such as reaching the age of sixty-five). Companies and governments essentially said, "If you do what I want you to do today, I'll give you money tomorrow."

Now, more than a hundred years after that first wave of pensioners, we have several generations of people who have actually been incentivized to put off their dreams until age sixty-five or later. With a promise in hand (from management or government or retirement planners) that life-after-work will be better, we crumple up our dreams like a paper ball and toss them out the window, hoping that the wind will blow those dreams back our way when we finally hit retirement.

The *ability* to retire is great! The *unintended consequence* of retirement planning, however, is that while people plan for future financial savings and investments (a good thing), they get it all mixed up with saving their dreams for later (a bad thing). Save your money, not your dreams!

In the bestselling book *The Four Hour Workweek*, Tim Ferris asks the thought-provoking question, "How do your decisions change if retirement isn't an option?" For the sake of argument, let's pretend that retirement does not exist. You work, and you work, and you work, and then, you die. If this were the case, would you truly wait another thirty or forty years to start implementing the ideas that are planted inside your head and heart *right now?* Would you wait another thirty or forty years to start living the life you truly want to live?

> *"Don't ever confuse the two, your life and your work. The second is only part of the first. Don't ever forget what a friend once wrote Senator Paul Tsongas when the senator*

decided not to run for reelection because he'd
been diagnosed with cancer: 'No man ever
said on his deathbed I wish I had spent more
time in the office.'"

—ANNA QUINDLEN, PULITZER PRIZE–WINNING AUTHOR

Retirement confusion has talked people in their *twenties* into believing that they need to wait until their *sixties* to do what they really have in mind with their lives!!!!! (Yes, five exclamation points!) What is that? *It is absurd.* But after interviewing too many people who fell into the retirement mentality trap, I feel a responsibility to warn you: it's a slippery slope, and it can happen to you.

CLARIFYING PRINCIPLES

RULE #1: Saving and investing money for the future = GOOD

RULE #2: Saving dreams (stupid ideas) for the future = BAD

What Do You *Really* Want?

As you consider your own plans for your life, your own stupid ideas, ask yourself if you've been waiting your whole life to do what you *really* want to do. Ask yourself if there's been an idea percolating through your mind that you feel you need to do something about, and how you might feel if someone else beat you to it. What if someone acted on your idea without you? What if you *never* get around to it?

Don't let that person be you. Those ideas that people mistakenly disregard as "stupid" or "bad timing" can become life-changing opportunities. Make it your personal responsibility to make ideas happen. When you decide, really decide, to move on ideas that you want to pursue, you'll no longer be the person that says:

"I'll do it later."

"Maybe someday."

"I wish I could, but I can't because . . ."

Those are the words of nonachievers and regret-mongers. Instead of wondering when you're finally going to start, decide to act today.

Don't get lost in waiting.

Don't live a life of regret.

Don't lose out on opportunities that can influence your life and the lives of others for good.

There is a great saying, often attributed to Abraham Lincoln, which poignantly reminds us, "Good things may come to those who wait, but only the things left by those who hustle."

"So what do we do? Anything. Something.
So long as we just don't sit there.
If we screw it up, start over.
Try something else.
If we wait until we've satisfied
all the uncertainties, it may be too late."

—LEE IACOCCA

PART II

The Time Has Come

It's as simple as that.

WILL I

REGRET IT

WHEN I'M

EIGHTY?

4

The Bezos Test:
Will I Regret It When I'm 80?

"Do not act as if thou wert going to live ten thousand years."
—MARCUS AURELIUS, ROMAN EMPEROR

Jeff had a secure, well-paying job, a job that made him happy. By a societal measure, the guy had it all. Everything, including a wickedly stupid idea.

So when he asked himself, "When I'm eighty, will I regret leaving Wall Street?" he countered his question with a more specific dream: "Will I regret missing a chance to be there at the beginning of the Internet?" When he assessed his current situation against the lure of his stupid idea, the choice was clear. He just had to jump ship. He got a loan from his mom and dad, hopped into his car with his wife, and drove from New York City to Seattle in order to start a website out of his garage. This is the story of Jeff Bezos, and the birth of Amazon.com.

I know what some of you are thinking: "Nice try. On

what planet was Amazon.com a stupid idea?" From a current market paradigm, nothing about Amazon.com is anywhere in the ballpark of stupidity (it's not even on the same continent). But in the mid-1990s, the Internet was nothing close to what it is today. Most people weren't comfortable with the Internet or confident in the reliability of the world of e-commerce. His idea was creative, it was innovative, and even Bezos himself called it "crazy"—all indicators, that within the framework of the mid-1990s, his idea definitely met the criteria for stupid as the New Smart.

> **"When I'm eighty, will I regret leaving Wall Street?"**

In an interview with the American Academy of Achievement, Bezos explains:

> I went to my boss and said to him, "You know, I'm going to go do this crazy thing and I'm going to start this company selling books online." This was something that I had already been talking to him about in a sort of more general context, but then he said, "Let's go on a walk." And we went on a two-hour walk in Central Park in New York City and the conclusion of that was this. He said, "You know, this

actually sounds like a really good idea to me, but it sounds like it would be a better idea for somebody who didn't already have a good job."

Did you catch that? Bezos had a good idea, even his boss thought so, but he was told it would have been a *better* idea for somebody who didn't already have a good job! Sometimes it's not the idea that's stupid, it's the idea within the context of the current situation.

We can learn a powerful lesson from Bezos's experience with starting Amazon.com. He said,

> If you can project yourself out to age 80 and sort of think, "What will I think at that time?" it gets you away from some of the daily pieces of confusion. You know, I left this Wall Street firm in the middle of the year. When you do that, you walk away from your annual bonus. That's the kind of thing that in the short-term can confuse you, but if you think about the long-term then you can really make good life decisions that you won't regret later.

What if Bezos had waited until a non-stupid time (a time when he didn't "already have a good job") to start Amazon? Judging by the magnitude of growth experienced in the world of e-commerce within such a consolidated period of time, his river may have run dry before he could float a single book down it! Instead, Bezos did the "crazy thing" and became a living legend, even gracing the cover of *Time* magazine in 1999 as "Person of the Year." Jeff Bezos changed the world as we knew it, all because he was stupid enough to start.

> *"It is not the critic who counts; not the man who points out how the strong man stumbles, or where the doer of deeds could have done them better. The credit belongs to the man who is actually in the arena, whose face is marred by dust and sweat and blood; who strives valiantly, who errs and comes up short again and again, because there is no effort without error or shortcoming; but who does actually strive to do the deeds; who knows the great enthusiasms, the great devotions; who spends himself in a worthy cause; who at the best knows in the end the triumph of high achievement, and who at worst, if he fails, at least fails while daring greatly, so that his place shall never be with those cold timid souls who know neither victory nor defeat."*
>
> —THEODORE ROOSEVELT

Where *Not* to Start

When I teach what I call the "Stupid Principles" to audiences or in private consultations, I'm asked this question more than almost any other: "I have so many ideas! What if I pick the *wrong one*?" Beware! You're in the quicksand of *paralysis by analysis,* and it has suffocated more great ideas than all the other potential stumbling blocks combined!

You can't let fear and indecision sink your creativity—they do not easily release their hold. Fear and indecision will stop you dead in your tracks every time. They'll keep you stuck where you already are; and you will start exactly *zero* of your beautifully stupid ideas.

Another temptation people face when trying to decide where to begin is to say, "Well, I guess I should just try them all and see what sticks." But then they flip right back around and say, "No, I must *focus*. Focus is the key!" These two conflicting thoughts can quickly freeze you in the realm between thought and action, and as a result, again, you'll find that *absolutely nothing happens at all.*

Here's the deal: If you're scared of choosing the wrong idea to start, you're going to keep yourself from starting altogether. And on the flip side, if you try to start *all* of your stupid ideas at once, you're bound to waste time, energy, and money (and go completely *loco* in the process). Plus, no matter how hard you focus, if you're laser-focused on the wrong activity or activities, your laser is going to end up burning a hole right through your potential for success.

You've got to be able to cut straight through all the

chaos and confusion in order to pinpoint where to begin. Start by familiarizing yourself with what I've termed "The Stupid Equation."

FUTURE REGRET = TODAY'S IMPERATIVE

Wouldn't it be amazing if you could travel into the future, see where you messed up, and then go back in time to rearrange things in order to make your future better? *You can.* If you can foresee regret, you can *mind-travel* to the future. If you can train yourself to mind-travel effectively, you can intentionally affect your future by doing something about it today.

The Bezos Test: Will I Regret It When I'm 80?

Question 1: Do you have a pressing thought or idea that simply won't go away?

What have you wanted to do for a while and plan or hope to get around to later? Perhaps these are ideas that you are deeply passionate about, but at some point you decided not to pursue them for one reason or another (not enough time, feeling underqualified, not enough money, a good idea for someone in a different life situation).

Take five to ten minutes and jot down as many of these thoughts as you can. (Consider doing this exercise in an e-mail to yourself, so you always have a searchable, date-stamped reference for later.)

Your list can be long or short. There are no rules here; simply do whatever works best for you. You may end up with a list of a hundred bullet points, or you could have just one thing that is really important to you.

_____

_____

_____

_____

Now, imagine your eightieth birthday. You're relaxing in your rocking chair on the porch, you pull out the list you just created, and you start thinking back over the years. You realize you didn't end up doing anything on that list. Some of the things you don't feel much concern or regret over, some things on the list make you laugh, but there are a few items written there that bring you a deep feeling of sadness and regret as you contemplate the joy and fulfillment that could have been yours (and your family's) if you'd only had the courage to try.

Question 2: Looking at your list, what would you regret *not* doing?

This should narrow your list down substantially.

_____

_____

_____

_____

Question 3: If you had only a short time to live, and you were required to rid yourself of all the things from your list except for three or four, which three to four ideas would remain?

This should further narrow down your list to only the things that truly are most important in your life.

_____

_____

_____

_____

Question 4: If you had to prioritize these few things in order from most important to least important, which order would you choose?

_____

_____

_____

_____

Congratulations!

You now know which stupid ideas are most important for you to focus on first.

> *"The common question that gets asked in business is, why? That's a good question, but an equally valid question is, why not?"*
>
> —JEFF BEZOS, FOUNDER OF AMAZON.COM

Additional Tips and Tricks

Stuck, or maybe just a little uncertain you've truly chosen the best idea of all? Anxiety over this part of the process is common. For many, the concept that you're actually *allowed* to do the things you're inherently passionate about is a new kind of thinking altogether. You've got to be patient with yourself as you adjust to this new paradigm.

Don't allow yourself to get so dammed up with fear about making the *wrong* decision that you are *unable to decide at all.* Quiet down, tune in, and trust your gut—go easy on yourself if overwhelming clarity doesn't immediately come. It's a process, and sometimes it takes time.

> If you're still in the boat of uncertainty and indecision, don't fret. Here are two more soul-searching (and admittedly somewhat melodramatic) questions that will help you further refine your list.
>
> 1. If this idea is the last thing I ever do, will it be something I'd be proud to be remembered by?
>
> 2. If I were forced at gunpoint to choose only one of these ideas, which one would it be?
>
> The urgency created by these two scenarios often serves to provide the clarity necessary to knock us free from indecision. If you really take these questions seriously, they can effectively shake your best ideas from the tree, and you'll quickly and confidently be able to determine which projects are most important to you.

Your stupid idea may or may not fit into the framework of a fantastic, end-of-life scenario, and that's okay. These questions aren't one-size-fits-all. They are simply a way to help you get started. You will have lots of ideas that are important and that coincide with different areas of your life. Whatever the question you choose to ask yourself to help you narrow things down, the concept will be the same.

For example, maybe you have a stupid idea that could potentially help your company reach a certain milestone. If so, ask yourself, "If our company doesn't reach that milestone by a certain date, will I regret having not shared or acted on my idea? Will I regret wondering if I could have made a difference? Will I have missed out on a once-in-a-lifetime, career-changing opportunity?" Or maybe you have a stupid idea that could help your community. If so, ask yourself, "If this issue in our community doesn't improve over the next year, is there a risk that something might happen (or not happen) that would cause me to regret keeping this idea to myself?" You could ask yourself similar questions about your family, your life, or your health, for example. The point is, you can modify the premise of the Bezos Test so that the questions work for your particular circumstance. Even a simple change in nuance might make the world of difference for your mental process.

"If at first the idea is not absurd, then there is no hope for it."

—ALBERT EINSTEIN

The Bezos Test in Action

One afternoon, my friend Jase drove into my driveway and ran over my seven-year-old son's longboard skateboard. Jase apologized profusely, and I told him not to worry about it. It wasn't a big deal, and really, it was my son's fault for leaving his board in the driveway in the first place.

A few days later, Jase came back to my house with a new skateboard deck that he had made by hand. He proceeded to remove the old wheels from the broken board and put them on the new deck. He told me how much he had enjoyed the board-making process. It had interested and energized him, and his excitement and fulfillment were written all over his face.

"Could I possibly start a skateboard company?" he asked me.

Jase knew this was a stupid idea for three reasons:

1. He wasn't a skater.

2. He didn't know anything about the skate industry.

3. He didn't have any capital available to invest in his dream.

However, the idea excited him too much to simply ignore. Only a few days later, he had turned his garage into a woodshop and was busily working on perfecting his custom skateboard decks, hoping to sell a few on the side.

One of Jase's clients from his day job had recently moved from Asia to Hawaii, and he visited Jase one day while he was plugging away in his makeshift skate lab. He asked Jase, "Why don't you have them manufactured in bulk? I have all the business connections already established, and I'll help you if you want to make me a partner."

Jase wasn't sure if he should take this little side project to the next level. After all, he had other pressing responsibilities (five of which were age eight and under). He consulted with me, and I told him about the Bezos Test. When he looked at things from that perspective, the choice was clear. Jase knew that, at age eighty, he would regret not investing the time to try to start a skateboard company.

Jase continued his regular work in the day, but in the afternoon or evening hours, he was hard at work in his garage, focused intently on perfecting his boards.

Before he knew it, he was meeting with manufacturers with his new partner in order to have the boards mass-produced. Less than a year later, Jaseboards were a hit, shipping boards out worldwide and even counting Costco Wholesale as one of its distributers.

Not only did a stupid mistake and a stupid idea create a new company, but Jase found a great friend in his new business partner, and he now leads a more fulfilling and purpose-driven life. I've known Jase nearly ten years, and I've never seen him light up the way he has since he started working on Jaseboards.

Why Not You?

You can apply the Bezos Test to any area in your life: finding a job, building a career, making money, pursuing marriage and family, focusing on health and fitness, undertaking entrepreneurial endeavors, leading a new project in your organization, seeking out educational opportunities, and on and on and on. No matter the area of focus, the formula is the same:

FUTURE REGRET = TODAY'S IMPERATIVE

The overarching goal is to determine which ideas are most aligned with your core values for your life, and then to simply *start*.

Stupid ideas have the power to change lives. Why not let one change yours?

5

The T.E.M. Gap: No Time, No Education, No Money = No Excuse

"Do what you can, with what you have, where you are."
—THEODORE ROOSEVELT

There was no funding for their venture. No government grants. No high-level connections. Not a single person on the team had an advanced degree or even a college education." From a practical standpoint, they had absolutely nothing they needed to achieve success.

No one believed in them and, in fact, they were referred to as no more or less than "a pair of crazy fools." At least that's what the lifeguards called them as they imitated the seagulls flying around the beach in Kitty Hawk, North Carolina. "We laughed about 'em among ourselves," one of the villagers later explained. But Orville and Wilbur Wright didn't care about the skepticism or even the scorn.

In reply to one reporter, the Wright brothers

commented, "The public can call us fakers or even crazy. We don't care. We know what we have got and others know, too." Yes, Orville and Wilbur Wright were determined to make that flying machine, no matter the odds, even if it meant "spreading their arms and twisting their wrists in imitation of the birds."

The Wright brothers didn't worry about their lack of resources, the impracticality of their goal, or the type of response they got from the community, the press, or even the world. They were unstoppable because they were completely focused on, and anchored by, the one thing they did have: a brilliantly stupid idea. Orville and Wilbur Wright had a stupid idea that they believed in so completely that they pressed forward boldly in the face of ridicule, scorn, and even the gravitational pull of the Earth, and those boys learned how to fly.

We All Have Excuses

In the last chapter, you identified your own, vitally important stupid idea(s). But chances are good that those same ideas were mulling around in your mind long before you started reading this book. So the pressing question is: Why haven't you started working on them yet?

Something in your life is taking precedence over those ideas, making it "stupid" for you to concentrate on them right now. The three most common excuses I hear in my consulting practice for postponing the initiation of stupid ideas are:

1. I don't have enough time.
2. I don't have enough education or experience.
3. I don't have enough money.

Here is the cold, hard fact of the matter. No matter how hard you work, no matter how much you study, no matter how much money you earn and tuck away, no matter (*insert your favorite excuses here*), there is still no guarantee that the stars will eventually align in the way you're waiting for them to. And for *most* of us, it's actually highly improbable that they ever will.

That knowledge shouldn't be discouraging. You have just been liberated! You have exactly zero reasons left to wait until later. You are as ready today as you're ever going to be, and with that understanding comes an empowering choice: You can overcome your circumstances or you can let your circumstances overcome you.

The Time, Education (Experience), Money Gap

Right now, there is likely a great divide between your inspired idea and your ability to take that *first step* toward success. In order to get yourself to the starting line, you've got to jump across the initial gap between your idea and green-light-go. I call this divide—this bottomless abyss—the time, education (experience), money gap (or the TEM Gap).

Using the excuse of a lack of time, education, or money (or anything else you can think up) will not only keep you stuck where you are but, even worse, it will actually make you feel *justified* in postponing your dreams. What's really happening here? You're buying into the limiting belief that no matter how badly you want to, no matter how deeply seated your passion, you simply can't start now. Your hands are tied by circumstance, and there's nothing in the world you can do about it.

Well, call the whaambulance, kids, because *Mama don't buy it.*

Time

First things first. If we're viewing time from a lifespan perspective, we will actually have *less* time later than we do right now. It's simple logic that each day we wait, we are left with less remaining time to do our dream work, and less time to live our happiest, most fulfilled lives.

> *"A year from now, you'll wish you started today."*
> —KAREN LAMB

If that's not a healthy enough dose of perspective, if that's not reason enough to kick things solidly into gear, take a moment to remember the common adage that has been whispered in your ear since infancy: "You are the future." Yes, *you* are that little boy or girl who, years ago, everyone was banking on to grow up and change the world. Well, it's actually happened. You are all grown up, but you are most certainly *not* the future. You are the now, and your "future" is today.

"Time Is Hard"

I once went to pitch a social entrepreneurial business venture at the office of a major venture capital firm. As I entered the building, I recognized a multimillionaire and well-known philanthropist on his way out. I later commented to the executive I was meeting about the person who had just left his office, and this is what he related to me:

"He wanted my time. Money is easy. Time is hard."

Time doesn't care how much money you accumulate. Time doesn't care how much education you have. Time doesn't care how long you wait for your life to settle down. Time will always be hard to find. So the way I see it, you can start now and reach for your dreams, or you can wait for later and hope that "later" doesn't prove to be too late. (P.S. Later, you'll have a whole new set of time-related issues to negotiate.)

Since I was a kid, I've enjoyed flipping through the

dictionary to learn new words and their origins. (I know. I've always been a little weird.) One day, in my late teens, I flipped to a page with the definition of a phrase I'd never heard before: Parkinson's Law. It stated: "Work expands so as to fill the time available for its completion." I laughed aloud as I remembered all my high school papers and projects that were never started until just before their deadlines. (Seriously sorry for the stress, Mom!)

Just like those horrible high school projects from days gone by, our dreams won't get started until they're due. But in this scenario, the teacher hasn't revealed the due date yet. Don't sit around twiddling your thumbs, assuming that time will expand eternally before you. Remember Gavin's Law. Life is short. Don't wait another day to start doing the things you really want to be doing, or to start living the life you truly want to live.

> If time were to take on human form, would she be
> your freedom fighter or your taskmaster?
> It's time to take back the reins.
> Don't sacrifice your life upon the altar of time.

Education and Experience

In 2007, I received an unexpected call from Stephen M. R. Covey, former CEO of FranklinCovey and author of the bestselling book, *The Speed of Trust*. He asked to meet with me. We sat down in his conference room, and Covey told me that after hearing me speak at a recent event he hoped I might consider coming to work for him presenting *Speed of Trust* trainings.

As soon as I scooped my jaw off the floor, I told him that, although I was incredibly flattered, I felt I was too young and inexperienced even to entertain the idea. "What would the gray hairs think?" Then, Covey taught me a priceless principle that would forever change my outlook on the nature of education and experience. He said, "Richie, experience is overrated. Some people say they have twenty years' experience, when, in reality, they only have one year's experience, repeated twenty times."

> **"Experience is overrated."**

That statement blew my mind and opened windows of opportunity all around me. In an instant, I felt free from the self-inflicted mental bondage I had created for myself about my age and my feelings of experience-based inadequacy. I suddenly realized that if something was important enough to me, if I was truly committed to achieving success, I could learn what I needed to know along the way! Nothing could have felt more empowering.

It's very important to note that Covey wasn't implying

that experience isn't important. Take a look at the way he elaborated on this concept in his book, *The Speed of Trust*.

> On the individual level, the problem is that many people aren't into the idea of continuous improvement. So they're working in a company—maybe they've been there for ten or fifteen years—but instead of having fifteen years of experience, they really have only one year of experience repeated fifteen times . . . As a result, they don't develop the credibility that would inspire greater trust and opportunity.

Just as valuable as experience, is an eagerness to learn and a willingness to constantly seek improvement to get the job done. Covey taught me that *authentic* experience is gained not by simply strapping yourself in and doing the time, but through constantly (and sincerely) seeking learning and improvement *along* the road to success.

I deeply value education and experience, of both the formal and the "lifelong learning" varieties. However, holding yourself back from starting your "real" life's work until you feel you finally have enough experience or education to actually begin is unwise. No matter how much you learn, you'll never have enough experience or education to anticipate every curveball that your life, your business, or your family will throw at you.

It's painful for me to imagine how many passionate dreamers and innovative thinkers have choked on their creative, potentially life-changing aspirations, while they waited to obtain enough experience to begin. The great author and creative director Paul Arden once said, "Experience is the opposite of being creative"—an intriguing argument that drives home a powerful point.

Anna Hargadon was a theater major determined to do something significant with her education while still in school. She wanted to start a project that involved theater and children with autism. After approaching her department chair and academic advisers, Anna received limited support. It seemed that because it was something new and nontraditional, there wasn't any room for it in undergraduate studies.

Despite her lack of experience and the lack of support from her advisers, Anna began anyway. Her project emphasized the connection between theater and practicing social interaction for children with autism. As Anna pursued her stupid idea, she made meaningful connections with industry experts and attended conferences that bolstered her confidence and passion for the field. Her project turned out to be a great success and, as a result, by the time Anna graduated from college, she had already developed an independent career working to help people with autism discover and develop their talents by participating in theater classes and productions.

Shortly after graduation, Anna received a grant to help schools create theater programs for children with autism. She also began working with an autism researcher to create a one-woman play, *Life, Love and Autism,* which chronicles the varied experiences and feelings of parents living with and loving children with autism. All of this meaning and success came into Anna's life because she wasn't afraid to start and she overcame her lack of experience along the way.

Education and experience certainly should not be viewed as staunch barriers to entry. Few people would ever achieve anything of genuine significance if that were the case. Seek continuous education and experience, yes, *and* start your inspired projects along the way.

Money

Oprah was born into poverty, raised in the inner city, and abused growing up. Today, she is one of the most powerful, influential, and wealthy people in world.

J.K. Rowling went from rags to riches, from being on welfare to making millions in just a few years with her mega-hit Harry Potter franchise. Rowling declared at a Harvard University commencement address, "Rock bottom became the solid foundation on which I rebuilt my life."

Steve Jobs felt guilty burning through his parents' life savings to get through college, so he dropped out, audited classes, and slept "on the floor in friends' rooms, returned Coke bottles for the 5¢ deposits to buy food with, and would walk the 7 miles across town every Sunday night to get one good meal a week at the Hare Krishna temple." Now Jobs is a modern-day legend. The Apple computer company he started in his parents' garage actually became "the most valuable company in history."

If starting dreams were dependent on your bank account, then we'd have no "rags to riches" stories. No Oprah. No J.K. Rowling. No Steve Jobs. These examples may be extreme, but they are also *real*. These remarkable individuals demonstrate that you don't have to wait for ideal financial circumstances before you start working toward your dreams. In fact, I'd wager that the necessity of pushing hard against those less-than-ideal circumstances is partially responsible for their vast success.

All these individuals had to do was make the simple choice to wait. All they had to say was, "This is just too hard. I'll wait and do it later," and the world would be a completely different place. Aren't we grateful they didn't choose to trade their legacy and their life's influence for a deceptive, convenient time (like retirement) to start inspiring others, writing books, or inventing computers?

For a moment, consider what the world would be like today without household names like Oprah, Harry Potter, or Apple. Whether you like them or not, no one can argue that the world we live in would be very different if they didn't exist. These distant public figures have made a personal impact on the lives of millions because they didn't wait to start creating the ideas they had in their hearts and minds until that elusive time when their financial circumstances would magically align with their goals.

Money Expands

After working in financial services over the years and reviewing hundreds of people's finances, I've noticed Parkinson's Law in action as it relates to the way many people handle money. Just as "work expands so as to fill the time available for its completion," so, too, does money expand so as to fill the expenses available. For example, without discipline, if a family's monthly disposable income is five hundred dollars a month, they will find a way to spend five hundred dollars a month. Increase that disposable income from five hundred to one thousand dollars, and they'll find a way to spend one thousand dollars a month. I found this tendency to be true no matter how much money the family made (unless they were strictly following some sort of saving or investing plan).

For example, in the 1970s and 1980s, Donald Trump amassed a massive fortune. However, in 1990, Trump faced an incredibly public financial ruin. The media was abuzz about Trump's financial situation during this trying time for him. *People* magazine reported that he needed to "limit his personal living expenses to $450,000 a month, which will mean cutting back by more than $100,000 his monthly outlay on such fripperies as $2,000 suits and the ministrations of the staff at his three homes."

The moral of the money story is this: It's not about the amount of money you do or do not have; it's how you view and use the money you have that matters.

The Art of Resourcefulness

Truthfully, if you think you don't have enough money to get started on your project, it can actually be quite a blessing! If you do start now, despite the lack of monetary abundance, necessity will dictate that you learn the art of resourcefulness in the form of bootstrapping. This process will require you to become intimately acquainted with the value of networking (learning to authentically connect with and effectively influence others). You'll also learn the value of partnering with others to get where you need to be (the concept of 1+1=3). Never underestimate the long-term value (or the power) of developing the art of resourcefulness.

In the future (when you have all the money you could ever want), the art of bootstrapping through networking, partnering with others, and of course, exercising frugality, will be critical to your sustainable success. You'll experience deep gratitude that you learned these invaluable lessons early, so you won't blow your fortune learning them the (extra) hard way later on.

The Bottom Line

You may tell yourself that in the future you'll have all the time you need, all the education you need, and all the money you need to finally get your project off the ground. If that's your mantra, you're already buying into the retirement mentality, and you're falling right into the Time-Education-Money Gap.

Every successful person has faced one, two, or all three of these obstacles (lack of time, education, and/or money) at one time or another on their journey toward success. No matter who they are, no matter the simplicity or complexity of the goal or their level of preparedness for the project as a whole, there is a point along the path when they will realize that the new project or goal is far more time intensive than they originally expected, or that there are aspects of the work they didn't anticipate and don't have the expertise to deal with, or that the project will cost more than originally planned. Successful people keep going anyway. Successful people don't use the obstacles of time, education, and money as excuses, and *neither should you.*

> **Note: Acting on the principles taught in Part III and Part IV will further help you overcome the Time-Education-Money Gap.**

PART
III

The Business of Stupid

IBM CONDUCTED a face-to-face study of more than fifteen hundred CEOs from sixty countries and thirty-three industries and identified creativity as the most important leadership quality for future success in times of complexity. The study explains, "Creative leaders invite disruptive innovation, encourage others to drop outdated approaches, and take balanced risks." Conventional wisdom has its limitations, and in today's fast-paced global economy, organizations demand creativity and unconventional thinking to maintain the competitive edge—organizations demand the New Smart.

If creativity really is the most crucial factor for future success, why aren't more people disrupting the status quo with new ideas? It's simple. The majority of people don't have the courage to push past stupid and engage the New Smart.

Creativity is at the heart of every stupid idea. In fact, it would be safe to say that more often than not, creativity and stupid are interchangeable. Stupid ideas come from a very powerful, creative space within our hearts and minds. The natural tendency is to recoil from these ideas, because everything inherent to that kind of creativity requires breaking away from the norm, going against the grain, and leaning into risk and fear. To many people, great creativity is just not worth the risk (or the discomfort)—particularly not within the firmly established culture of an organization as a whole.

This is the very real challenge presented to unconventional thinkers: the general population, not to mention the typical organization, isn't consciously aware that unconventional is what they really need. Few are willing to put their money, or their jobs, on the line for an unconventional idea. This is the very reason that the greatest in innovation and creativity are so quickly labeled "stupid" and rarely have the opportunity to come into conventional (and profitable) fruition. However, in order to compete in today's aggressive economy, fostering creativity within your organization isn't just a nice idea, it's a necessity for success.

The willingness to be a champion for stupid ideas is the key to greater creativity, innovation, fulfillment, inspiration, motivation and success. Making space for the New Smart in business and in life is not only possible, it's essential in order to maintain the competitive edge, foster greater fulfillment, and achieve meaningful and sustainable success. Within the framework of your organization (or your life) as a whole, you simply cannot afford not to make space for stupid.

Don't get stuck at Model T

6

Innovation and the Stupid Loop: Don't Get Stuck at Model T

"Business men go down with their businesses because they like the old way so well they cannot bring themselves to change."
—HENRY FORD

Making unconventional decisions was part of Henry Ford's DNA. Before his success with automobiles, he tested a gasoline-powered "quadricycle" by driving it through the streets of Detroit. "And whenever Henry stopped, enthusiastic crowds swarmed around him and his vehicle. Several people . . . [yelling] out, 'Crazy Henry!' 'Yes, crazy,' Henry would [reply], tapping the side of his head with a finger, 'crazy like a fox.' He knew he was one step closer to producing a car for the masses." Eventually, he did just that.

Powered by enthusiasm and anchored to his goal by a deeply held conviction, he used his many failures as stepping-stones, instead of as stumbling blocks, to move him toward his eventual success. And successful he was.

Ford's Model T was so successful in fact that he sold more than fifteen million of them, and at one point, half of all cars in the world were Fords.

> *"Many men are afraid of being considered fools. But it is not a bad thing to be a fool. . . . The best of it is that such fools usually live long enough to prove that they were not fools—or the work they have begun lives long enough to prove they were not foolish."*
> —HENRY FORD

Ford continually embraced stupid. One poignant example is when he astonished the world in 1914 by increasing his laborers' wage to five dollars a day. This more than doubled the previous pay rate of most of his workers. In response to this unconventional decision, "Ford was hailed as the friend of the worker, as an outright socialist, or as a madman bent on bankrupting his company." Stockholders considered him reckless, but despite commotion and resistance, Ford stuck with his stupid pay raise. His innovation proved successful; it increased employee retention, secured Ford the best mechanics in the area, and raised productivity across the board. Ford laughed all the way to the bank when company profits doubled that year, rising from 30 to 60 million dollars. Ford later reflected, "The payment of five dollars a day for an eight-hour day was one of the finest cost-cutting moves we ever made."

Over time, however, Ford's "crazy like a fox" methods normalized within the market. *Forbes* explains what happened as the automotive industry matured:

> The market began to shift; price and value ceased to be paramount factors. Styling and excitement suddenly counted to the customer. Even though the Model T cost a mere $290 in the mid-twenties, dealers clamored for a new Ford that would strike the fancy of the more demanding and sophisticated consumers.
>
> But Henry Ford refused even to consider replacing his beloved Model T. Once, while he was away on vacation, employees built an updated Model T and surprised him with it on his return. Ford responded by kicking in the windshield and stomping on the roof. "We got the message," one of the employees said later. "As far as he was concerned, the Model T was god and we were to put away false images."

Henry Ford literally "smashed" and "stomped" on the efforts of his intrapreneurial employees to make improvements to the Model T, while the rest of the world watched Ford's market share plummet until it was swallowed up by General Motors.

Why didn't Ford change? Well, why would he? His

original crazy ways worked. He had millions and millions of successful sales behind him. Arguably, Ford was king, and the Model T was his throne. By Ford's measure of success, his internal systems were essentially perfect and had been proven for nearly two decades.

The Stupid Loop

Stupid goes in a loop. It's cyclical. Like Ford and his Model T, if your stupid project becomes successful, it will likely become accepted, then considered smart, and then standardized, and eventually, *normal*.

Whoops. Normal is where innovation goes to die. Normal isn't new. People *like* "normal," but they *love* "new."

According to the Stupid Loop, a successful stupid project will become smart and even accepted and celebrated by the masses (or the niches). However, once stupid normalizes, you have to ask yourself, "Do I stay the same, for better or worse, or do I innovate—return to stupid—for better or worse?" Understanding the Stupid Loop, and why innovation is so vitally important, helps you develop the ability to check the pulse of the environment around you and adapt accordingly.

Essentially, the Stupid Loop is a formula for innovation. Innovation plus motivation equals sales. You must innovate in order to motivate consumers to keep buying

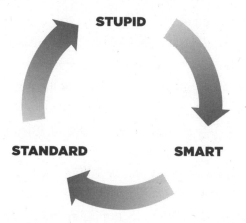

into your products and services. Think of the number of boy bands that come and go, or the catwalk fashion trends that appear and then disappear just as quickly, or the exercise trends that weave in and out of the mainstream. Consumers are constantly searching for something new to love. If you become too married to your stupid idea and refuse to evolve in the way the market demands, the New Smart can quickly become an unhealthy form of stupid, and it may die altogether.

While we're on the subject of unhealthy stupid, let's expand our definition of the concept to better illustrate how it affects our ability to maintain course along the Stupid Loop. Drawing from James E. Welles's book, *Understanding Stupidity*, the label of unhealthy stupid "requires the activity to be maladaptive, in that it is in the worst interest of the actor, and specifically done to prevent adaptation to new data or existing circumstances." Henry Ford and his unyielding commitment to his Model T are a prime example of an unwillingness to adapt to a changing environment and his story illustrates a phenomenon that plagues the economy at large.

We've all encountered people or businesses that refuse to adapt to new data or existing circumstances. Generally, this rigidity and unwillingness to adapt is born of fear. We fear the potential cost—in terms of monetary resources as well the emotional, mental, logistical, and time-related costs associated with change. We are afraid, and so we determine that it's stupid to stir things up, stupid to make that change. Not only is change-avoidance an unhealthy form of stupid, it can be downright dangerous, lulling us into a false belief that we are in fact being smart by staying where we are.

You have to be vigilant in order to stay relevant. If you remember nothing else from this chapter, remember this: if an entrepreneur, an intrapreneur, or a business leader stops leaning into stupid, doesn't embrace necessary change and continuous improvement, and doesn't have the courage to start fresh when necessary, he risks obsolescence. He risks setting the stage for others to swoop in and steal the show with their own amazingly stupid (and adaptive) innovations. He risks becoming extinct or, worse, irrelevant.

Live in Permanent Beta

How do we avoid becoming extinct? How do we ensure that we remain relevant? Reid Hoffman, cofounder and chairman of LinkedIn.com, suggests that we all live in "permanent beta"—that we "never stop starting" and "get busy livin', or get busy dyin'." Hoffman proposes that living in perpetual beta allows you to be nimble, invest in yourself, build your network, take intelligent risks, and "make uncertainty and volatility work to [your] advantage." It's a "mind-set brimming with optimism because it celebrates the fact that you have the power to improve yourself and, as important, improve the world around you." Do you hear that? YOU have the power. If you want to stay relevant and keep from becoming extinct, consider yourself liberated. The power is yours.

Many Internet companies (like Gmail or Amazon) begin in "beta" and stay there for years, constantly adding new "beta" features. "Web 2.0 applications are re-released, re-written and revised on an ongoing basis," and in today's ever-changing world, you need to have the flexibility to rerelease, rewrite, and revise yourself as you work toward achieving and sustaining success.

> *"Permanent beta is essentially a lifelong commitment to continuous personal growth."*
> —REID HOFFMAN, COFOUNDER AND CHAIRMAN
>   OF LINKEDIN

In order to survive, in order to *thrive,* you've got to commit to continuous reevaluation, continuous improvement, and continuous innovation—in other words, you've got to commit to continually embrace the New Smart.

Don't Get Stuck at Model T

One of the primary reasons GM overtook Ford was because GM embraced what they called "planned obsolescence" and "regularizing change" by rolling out new cars every year. GM understood that constantly returning to stupid—constantly innovating—is critical in order to stay relevant within a competitive market.

Henry Ford's initial knack for commotion, invention, and challenging the status quo was so wildly successful that the vibrant and innovative change he had originally pioneered had become rigid and unmovable. Stupid brilliance had morphed nearly imperceptibly into stubborn foolishness, until eventually Ford was forced to return to something stupid or fall off the map.

"By 1926, T sales had plummeted, and the realities of the marketplace finally convinced Henry Ford that the end was at hand." At that point, Ford finally loosened his grip and courageously returned to stupid. He sent his workers home, shut down his Highland Park factory for six months, and went on to design the Model A, which "was a success from its launch in December 1927, and placed the company on sound footing again."

Don't get stuck at Model T. If you want to stay relevant, constantly (and courageously) return to stupid.

Experiment.

THEN MOVE FORWARD
OR MOVE ON.

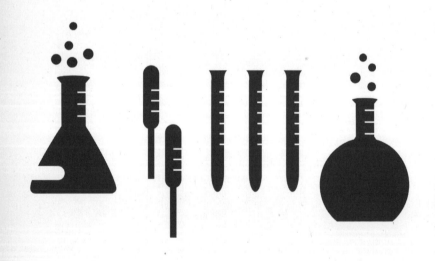

7

Stupid Projects:
How One Thing Leads to Another

"All life is an experiment.
The more experiments you make the better."
—RALPH WALDO EMERSON

In 2002, Darren Rowse hit "publish" on a blog for the first time. It was the early days of blogging, and Rowse was a pioneer in this vast new frontier of the World Wide Web. But at the time, he certainly didn't see it that way. He started a blog, the first of many that would follow, primarily out of curiosity. This "blogging thing" as he later called it, was more or less a fun experiment. At worst, he'd have a bit of fun, and at best, perhaps he could gain a new hobby and make some new connections in the process.

At the time, Rowse was trying to save money for a wedding, pay off his modest car, and put himself through college, so he was working three jobs just to make ends meet. His heavy load left little time for his new hobby, and over the next twelve months, nothing much changed in that regard. Posts were sporadic, and his blog was still visited mostly by friends from church, although it had also started to gain readership in the "emerging church circles."

As hosting costs began to escalate as a result of this small jump in readership, Rowse started to look for ways to cover the hard costs associated with his project. If the blog could simply cover its own costs, and perhaps bring in enough to pay for a customized blog design, that would be sufficient. Rowse started experimenting with AdSense and over the next few months, he saw a slow but steady increase in his daily profit average. In his own words,

> I quickly discovered that my hope of covering my expenses was a realistic one. . . . December saw daily earnings hit $6 per day, January $9, February $10 and March $15. Hardly big dollars, but I began to wonder what would happen if I saw the same sorts of increases in income over a longer period of time. By that I don't mean adding $2-$3 to the daily average per month, but what would happen if I could sustain 30%, 40% or even 50% growth each month. I began to think in terms of exponential growth.

From this point in Rowse's little experiment, one thing led quickly and measurably to another. In April, his daily earnings averaged $20; May, $32, and by June, he was averaging $48 per day from the side project he still managed in his free time.

Then came his moment of truth. A seed was planted in his mind that he simply could not shake. Yup, Rowse was hit by a stupid idea. He relates:

> This was a bit of a freaky moment for both [my wife] "V" and myself. Neither of us had started a small business and while I've always had something of an entrepreneurial spirit we are both fairly conservative people in many ways and while the figures indicated that there was potential on many levels it just seemed plain weird. I mean who makes their income blogging?

After nineteen months of experimenting, Rowse decided to commit two days of his work week to professional blogging. He recalls:

> Needless to say we didn't really tell too many people of our decision. When we did tell just a few family members and friends there were plenty of raised eyebrows and lots of comments like "That's nice but are you going to get a real job?" and "How's your little hobby business going?"

But despite the lack of understanding and/or support he received from others, Rowse leaned into his fear and acted on his stupid idea by starting small and building on his incremental success. He continued to experiment with different types of blogs, subjects, and styles, and he tested different ways to monetize his sites in order to determine what worked best. (At one point, he was managing twenty blogs at the same time!)

> "We are both fairly conservative people in many ways and while the figures indicated that there was potential on many levels it just seemed plain weird."

By 2005, Rowse had made the leap to full-time blogger. His little experiment had become a *full-time experience*. His initial growth was slow and steady. Over time, that growth accelerated and has continued to sustainably increase in depth and breadth ever since. Rowse's network of blogs now earns him a seven-figure income; his company b5media started over 300 blogs, received $2 million in venture capital and was recently acquired. He has also now become a popular author and speaker.

Rowse is best known for two sites: Problogger.net, which teaches professional blogging tips and is consistently listed as one of the top blogs in the world, and Digital-Photography-School.com, which is a massive online digital photography educational site with over 4 million visitors per month.

Overcoming the Psychology of Stupid: Moving from Idea to Project Phase

In order to give your stupid idea legs, you've got to first overcome the psychology of stupid. By their very nature, stupid ideas are often unconventional. Because of this, there is no existing road map designed to take us from "point A" (stupid idea) to "point Z" (stupid success). This lack of certainty causes us to become so overcome by our big-picture goals that we can't decipher where to begin.

Let's use Darren Rowse as an example. If his initial goal had been to earn a seven-figure income by blogging, chances are good that the complexity of that goal would have been so overwhelming that he wouldn't have known how or where to begin. And when we can't determine where to begin, more often than not, we don't begin at all.

The overwhelming psychology of stupid is overcome by breaking our big-picture goals into smaller, more manageable projects—projects that have a beginning and an end. Suddenly the very ideas that we didn't think we could possibly begin don't seem nearly as daunting. This simple change in identification transforms an abstract thought into an actionable task or assignment.

> It's much easier to get yourself and others
> behind a *project*—with a beginning and an end—
> than it is to get yourself and others behind an
> abstract, non-actionable *idea*.

For example, if you want to start a blog, then the script "I want to start a blog" should transform into "working on the Blog Project" or "working on the *(insert your name here)* Blog Project." If you want to start a dog farm, your script should change from "I want to start a dog farm" to "I'm working on the Dog Farm Project."

Projects Increase Overall Fulfillment

Projects lead not only to a greater chance for success, they provide greater fulfillment along the way. In the book *Personal Project Pursuit: Goals, Action, and Human Flourishing,* the authors draw from a remarkable amount of research to demonstrate "how personal projects can illuminate and enhance human flourishing, from psychological well being to physical health." The following quote from the book illustrates the authors' findings as it relates to the positive effects of personal projects within the framework of an organization. They state:

> In the final analysis, personal projects provide
> meaning, structure, and community in the lives

of people in organizations, and they also have impacts on those organizations. Personal projects, in short, are acts that have impacts and leave imprints. Personal projects, in this sense, are not merely personal. They are the connective tissue that keeps organizations functioning, for better or for worse.

Over a three-year period, I consulted the revenue-generating arm of a nonprofit organization. This organization had been running in the red, and I was hired to help the group generate profits so that they could become self-sustaining. I decided to experiment with personal projects that met the mission of the organization to see what would happen. Individuals created projects they were interested in, set deadlines to begin and end, started small, and built upon simple, incremental successes.

I observed a significant shift in overall profitability when employees were given projects in which they felt a sense of ownership and autonomy. Not only did department profitability increase, but also employees were suddenly engaged and enthusiastic about their work. Creativity increased as a result, and the entire department culture shifted. It is ironic to note that before personal projects were introduced, the group had been working in silos, with nearly no employee integration. As a natural by-product of the newly introduced personal projects, employees were suddenly invigorated and eager not only to complete their own tasks, but also to collaborate and help everyone else's projects succeed as well.

While we have been discussing personal projects within the framework of an organization, it is important to note that the results could be the same in *any* aspect of life. Personal projects, intrapreneurial projects, and entrepreneurial projects provide a sense of purpose and structure to our lives and can breathe new life into our organizations.

One Thing Leads to Another: How a Simple Project to "Make Caine's Day" Turned into Much, Much More

When Nirvan Mullick walked into Smart Parts Auto in East Los Angeles one afternoon, looking for a used handle for his 1996 Corolla, he walked right into the start of a project that would change his life, and the life of a nine-year-old boy, forever. As Mullick discovered, Smart Parts Auto was also home to an elaborate do-it-yourself arcade, comprised of a bunch of cardboard boxes and built by a boy named Caine. Mullick was Caine's first and only customer in months.

So impressed by Caine's attitude and the amazing attention to detail he had put into his cardboard arcade, Mullick, a filmmaker, decided to "make Caine's day" by producing a short film about Caine's Arcade.

With permission from the boy's father, Mullick organized a surprise flash mob at Caine's Arcade. The news of the surprise went viral, and over one hundred people came to play at Caine's Arcade—even NBC news attended the event.

The residual effects of this simple film project are astonishing. Within the first day the video was posted online, a total of $60,000 in scholarship money was raised for Caine. A week later, a dollar-for-dollar $250,000 funding grant from the Goldhirsh Foundation was set up to help fund the Caine's Arcade Imagination Foundation—designed "to find, foster, and fund creativity and entrepreneurship in more kids like Caine." Caine also received the Latino Spirit Award at the California State Assembly in Sacramento, and became the youngest speaker at Cannes Lions international festival of creativity.

As for Nirvan Mullick, he says, "This has opened up a lot of doors for me. There are people offering feature film deals based on Caine's Arcade. There are some series projects in development. . . . It's been pretty overwhelming. . . . I'm still figuring out what's happening here."

As we overcome the psychology of stupid by starting projects, one thing leads to another, sometimes in miraculous ways. Mullick was looking for a handle for his car door, when he decided to start a simple project with the solitary aim of making a kid's day. He never could have anticipated what would happen as a result.

Above and beyond anything else, personal projects get us moving. Because they generally require less in terms of time and other resources, they help us successfully close the Time-Education-Money Gap and start and maintain momentum toward our big-picture goals. In the end, personal projects may lead somewhere better than we ever could have dreamed.

How to Turn a Free Project into a Paying Gig

Chris Bennett had a well-paying job in Internet marketing consulting for small businesses. He loved the work he was doing, but he knew he eventually wanted to be his own boss. He started a variety of entrepreneurial ventures on the side, all in hopes of reaching his goal of becoming independent.

In one such entrepreneurial venture, Bennett dabbled in real estate investing, and when he lost everything but the shirt on his back, he decided it was time to reevaluate his process. He wondered if he was failing at these projects simply because his heart wasn't really in them to begin with. He decided to experiment. Instead of trying to make money by doing things he didn't like (conventional smart), he decided to give his services away for free, doing something that he loved (new smart).

A friend of his owned a small, marginally successful, local catering company. After Bennett took over their on-line marketing (a project he loved), they went from three to five calls a week to five to seven calls a *day*. Only a year later, the company had grown to become the second largest catering company in the state.

What happened next was interesting. Out of nowhere, other companies began contacting Bennett, inquiring about his services. Suddenly, he was a trusted, experi-enced Internet marketer. Chris Bennett's experiment had paid off. Not only had he proved his passion for Internet marketing, he now knew he could turn his passion into a profitable business.

From this experiment, Bennett's company, 97th Floor, was born. Seven years later, 97th Floor is work-ing with several *Fortune 100* companies and Bennett is a sought-after speaker all over the world on the subject of Internet marketing.

Bennett offers this advice to others, "Just start some-thing. . . . The first thing people say after starting on an idea is always, 'I only wish I'd started sooner!'"

Experiment with Stupid Projects

Projects are a wonderful way to experiment with your stupid ideas, because with a small project, the stakes are considerably lower than they are with a big-picture goal.

Projects allow us to experiment and determine what works and what doesn't. They also allow us room to fail and modify our ideas as necessary to achieve eventual success.

With an experiment, you can test as many ideas as you can, as fast as you want, and then go with the methods that are most effective. Consider how Mark Zuckerberg generates innovation at Facebook. *Fast Company* magazine once asked Zuckerburg, "How do you innovate?" He responded,

> A lot of people think innovation is just having a great idea. But a lot of it is just moving quickly and trying a lot of things. So, at Facebook we've really built our whole company and our culture around this. We do things like ship code every single day. And, um, we have this tradition of having hack-a-thons—which are events where all of our engineers and really the whole company get together and stay up all night just building things. Whatever they want. Not what they're doing for work. Just trying things out and innovating.

Stupid projects like the kind Zuckerberg promotes at Facebook spur innovation, and sometimes those innovative ideas stick.

Google is another prime example. As part of their mission, not only do they listen to every idea that comes through "on the theory that any Googler can come up with the next breakthrough," but they allow time for their employees to experiment with personal projects. "We offer our engineers '20-percent time' so that they're free to work on what they're really passionate about." The result of personal projects and experiments in areas that truly interest their employees are impressive, to say the least. For example, ideas like "Google Suggest, AdSense for Content and Orkut are among the many products of this perk."

Do you think you would you be more likely or less likely to test one of your so-called "stupid ideas" in an environment like the one Google strives to create? My money's on "more likely," and you can facilitate the same kind of environment in or outside of almost any organization.

Experiment with stupid projects and see what works. It's better to find out now if your idea is a flop (when the stakes are low) than to wait your whole life and find out your idea is a failure (when the stakes are high).

Try it out yourself. Test your idea with an experimental project. See what works and what doesn't. Then move forward or move on.

Use Personal Projects to Overcome Obstacles and Achieve Big-Picture Dreams

Over a consolidated period of time, Lara Casey left her lucrative yet unfulfilling job in New York City, underwent a painful divorce, lost her childhood home to

Hurricane Ivan, and nearly lost her only brother after he severed his spinal cord in a snowboarding accident.

As her life seemed to unravel around her, Casey refused to be overcome. She recalls, "I was at rock bottom. There was no place to go but *somewhere*." Over time, as she continued to put one foot in front of the other, things began to improve. Within a matter of months, Casey had met her soul mate, remarried and landed her dream job in California. But it was the height of the war in Iraq, and her new husband was suddenly deployed for an eight-month tour of duty. So Casey returned home to Florida to live with her parents and bide her time until her husband returned home.

"I couldn't watch the news," Casey recalls. "I waited by my phone day and night. I needed a project to keep my mind occupied. One night, I found myself dreaming of pretty things—anything to keep my mind off of bomb threats—and I decided to mock up a wedding magazine cover on my little PC."

Before she knew it, Casey was dreaming up photo shoots and looking up domain names. Because it was her only lifeline to sanity, Casey threw herself full force at this new project. "I thought I'd just print a tiny run and put it in local grocery stores, churches and bridal shows. God had a different plan." One thing led to another, and before Casey knew it, a full-fledged magazine was born!

Despite being hit by obstacle after obstacle, including a "scary" cease and desist order from a major publishing company, Casey prevailed. "The first issue of 'Southern Weddings Magazine' debuted to RAVE reviews," Casey recalls. "It was a phenomenal success and we sold out in 3 months. We sold 30% above the national average with that first issue. Readers were delighted. Sponsors were thrilled. Our distribution agents were elated." That same growth and success has been sustained for five years running with no sign of slowing down.

Casey has sustained her success by doing things on her own terms. Rather than being bought out by some big conglomerate, she has continued to approach Southern Weddings as a simple project. "We're not corporate or owned by some big publishing house. WE do the layout, write the editorial, organize the advertising— and everything else—ourselves. We are self-published, which nowadays is a rarity in print. We're really, really small. We never want to grow to the point where we can't give personal attention to what matters most. We are really grateful for that."

When I asked Casey what advice she had for others, she said,

How do you start a powerful thriving business? How do you get out of "overwhelmed" and start really living? You walk—sometimes through mud, jagged rocks, thick weeds, thorns, and on thin ice. But you will get to the other side, because you are walking through it. If you do not walk, you will not get to the other side.

I am not more extraordinary than anyone else. You were given gifts that were meant to be shown to the world. Stand up and put one foot in front of the other, right now. Step strongly. No mistakes, only lessons. Plant those feet on the ground and walk. You have this.

Commit

"You have this"—you do. No more waiting. If you keep overcomplicating your dreams, you'll never learn how wonderful it feels to actually step into them. Take a deep breath, and simply experiment with what's right in front of you by starting a stupid project. It's time to blaze your own trail. It's time to start living your dreams.

Making your stupid idea happen won't be easy. You have to be committed. Not halfway committed—you need to commit 100%. At times, you may stand all alone in your efforts to engage the New Smart, but standing alone is part of standing out, and standing out is often what it takes to inspire meaningful change—and it's all a part of embracing stupid.

"1984" is a legendary Apple commercial that ran during the 1984 Super Bowl. *TV Guide* hailed it as "the greatest commercial of all time." But the story behind the story is that the advertisement almost didn't make it on the air. The ad was intended to highlight the launch of the Macintosh personal computer, but not even once did the commercial show the product. Instead, the advertisement showed a woman, running with a sledgehammer, smashing an image of "Big Brother," reminiscent of George Orwell's book *1984*. The board at Apple wasn't thrilled. In fact, when Steve Jobs presented it to them, they "thought it was the worst commercial they had ever seen."

"Jobs was beside himself." He went to cofounder, Steve Wozniak, and showed him the ad. Wozniak "thought it was the most incredible thing." Jobs told Wozniak about the board's decision to scrap the ad for the Super Bowl time slot and explained that they consequently needed to sell the air time. But Wozniak was committed. He asked the cost of the Super Bowl slot, and when Jobs said it was $800,000, Wozniak replied, "Well, I'll pay half if you will."

In the end, Jobs and Wozniak didn't have to pony up the money for the ad, but they were completely prepared to, and *that's* commitment. That's 100%.

Embracing stupid as the New Smart means

committing to follow through with your stupid projects, committing to give them your 100%.

Chances are, you won't have to cough up $800,000 to run an ad during the Super Bowl, but there will be obstacles. It's part of the process of experimenting; it's part of blazing your own trail. But that's the beauty of a project in the first place—you don't have to commit to *forever,* it has a beginning and an end. Projects are a wonderful opportunity to ensure you're on the right path, but unless you commit to follow your project through to completion, even when the going gets rough and you're tempted to jump ship, you'll forever wonder what could have potentially been just around the next bend.

"A pessimist sees the difficulty in every opportunity; an optimist sees the opportunity in every difficulty."

—Winston Churchill

PART
IV

Making It Happen

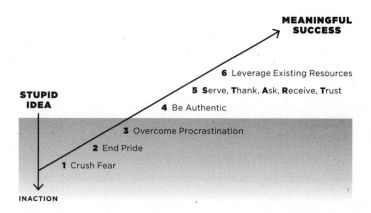

TO ACCELERATE SUCCESS, we must get as close to our dreams as possible, as soon as possible. The principles introduced in this section help bridge the gap between where we currently stand, and where we ultimately want to be. When authentically embraced, these principles help us to identify and perform the *right kind of work*—the work that makes our specific goals possible—*as soon as possible.*

Principles are commonly believed to be fundamental truths—"the foundation for a system of belief or behavior"—however a principle is much, much more than that. The Latin root for *principles* is *principium* meaning "source," and *princeps* or *princip* meaning "first" or "chief." Thus a principle is not merely a fundamental truth, but principles must serve as the very *first source* of every decision we make along the road to success. If embodied in all facets of business and life, the principles taught in this section will serve as a rock solid foundation for the meaningful, purpose-driven, sustainable success you seek.

The intent of these principles is to help you get out of your shell, get into the scene, and make dreams happen. Together, these principles will help you overcome the Time-Education-Money Gap and help turn your stupid idea into your happy reality.

1. Get Out of Your Shell

- Overcome Fear
- Overcome Pride
- Overcome Procrastination
- Be Authentic

These four principles work together to help move a stupid idea from inception to sustainable action. To illustrate, imagine what happens to a chicken that stays inside its egg. (It dies.) Likewise, there is a metaphorical egg that keeps us trapped. We must break through these damming barriers to success in order to reclaim our confidence and our ability to act on what matters most to our most meaningful success. Until we break free from the comfort of that egg, our most authentic goals and desires for ourselves are suffocated within its confines.

2. Get into the Scene: The 5 Actions of the New Smart

- **S**erve
- **T**hank
- **A**sk
- **R**eceive
- **T**rust

START is an acronym that stands for Serve, Thank, Ask, Receive, and Trust. When we genuinely START, we embody proven, timeless principles of connection, credibility and contribution. By authentically STARTing, we build our *inner circle of success* (or trusted network of people) and diligently lay the groundwork that allows us to effectively spur a groundswell when the time is right. START will help you connect with others, gain credibility and contribute to the world in significant ways.

3. Make Dreams Happen
- Leverage Existing Resources

Once we've broken out of our shell and created a trusted network with the power of START, we're prepared to leverage existing resources in order to maximize efforts and propel us toward our meaningful goals—more effectively than we ever could otherwise. In my study of success through starting something stupid, I have found time and time again that when these principles are authentically engaged as the *first, governing sources of behavior,* they accelerate and enhance our ability to turn a so-called "stupid" idea into New Smart success.

These principles are not gimmicks or maps or systems or shortcuts. Those types of plans are often shallow and superficial and begin to fall apart when we hit even the smallest bump in the road. Rather, these principles are a way of life. Living them helps us to not only accelerate our success, but to build a solid framework that will prepare us to effectively respond when unexpected obstacles appear before us. When authentically embraced, these principles propel us toward meaningful, purpose-driven, sustainable success.

"All our dreams can come true,
if we have the courage to pursue them."

—WALT DISNEY

8

Crush Fear:
How to Turn High Fear into
High Achievement

"Do one thing every day that scares you."
—ELEANOR ROOSEVELT

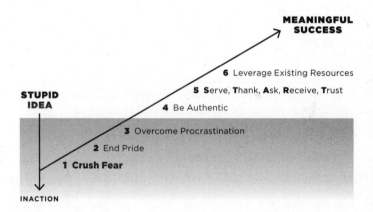

Andy Pierce walked past the "Danger: No Swimming" signs posted along the shore and negotiated his way through the pounding six-foot shore break. He had his eye on the twenty-foot waves at the horizon. Only a handful of guys were braving the waves at Sunset Beach that afternoon, but even though he paddled out completely alone, Pierce experienced total confidence. These waves were smaller than the ones he'd ridden at Waimea only the day before.

He positioned himself in the lineup just as a set of giant waves came roaring in from the outside break. The wind was so strong that he had to paddle harder than usual, taking extra strokes just to generate enough speed to get into the wave. He wasn't quite fast enough. He paddled in and got his feet on the board, but he was much too high on the wave. The lip of the wave grabbed Pierce and pitched him down into the flats, where a mass of water crashed over him. Fortunately, he resurfaced and was able to get back on his board.

The fall didn't shake him; it only made him *more* determined to catch his next wave. The second wave came. This one was bigger, heavier, and even more powerful than the first. Again, as he stood on the board, the wind began to pitch him forward, but this time he kept his footing. He dropped about fifteen feet to the water's surface and, as he landed, his board shot out from beneath him.

The water ripped him up around the crest of the wave and then pounded him down over the falls—like being thrown over a violent waterfall. The instant he crashed into the explosive white water, his surfboard came flying down fast from above. The edge of the board

slammed into his right leg like an axe, chopping his fe-
mur in two, and sending indescribable, excruciating pain
throughout his entire body.

After being pinned underwater for what seemed to
him to be eternity, Pierce came up for air and tried to
yell for help. For a moment he saw another surfer in the
distance, but he wasn't certain if that person had seen or
heard him, and either way more waves were coming—fast.

Pierce floated helplessly in the middle of the impact
zone as wave after wave pummeled him, each one pin-
ning him underwater for terrifying periods of time. As he
related, "I had no idea what to do. I remember thinking, 'I
can't believe this is happening; this doesn't happen to me,
it happens to other people.'" Pierce felt helpless, alone,
afraid, and confused. He recalls what happened next,

> When the next wave came, I'd been pushed in
> closer to shore, but I was still about two hundred
> yards or so from the beach. I grabbed my board and
> lay down on it. At this point, I realized no one was
> coming. I was going to have to get in all by myself,
> or drown. That's when a wall of whitewash nailed
> me. I felt my severed leg whirling around beneath me
> like a helicopter propeller. The pain was unfathom-
> able. Then I saw someone paddle up beside me. He
> ditched his board and said, "Let's go in."

As luck would have it, his rescuer was Jamie Mitchell—ten-time world paddleboard champion and Australian lifeguard. But even with Mitchell's impressive level of expertise, getting Pierce to shore was no picnic. They were still in the impact zone, and as they paddled, wave after wave hit them. The waves pushed them underwater over and over again. The power of the water whirled the surfers upside down and around in circles, but "Jamie pinned me to the surfboard," Pierce said, "by grabbing the rails and holding tight. He never let go."

With the help of other lifeguards and surfers who paddled to their aid, Pierce finally washed up on the shore. "I was alive," he told me, with as much awe and wonder in his voice as if the entire adventure had unfolded earlier that very day. "I was alive."

If you were Andy Pierce, would you ever surf again?

Within weeks, Pierce was back in the water, and only a few months after that, he was back to surfing big waves (only now with a shiny metal pole in his leg). He has been catching massive waves off various coasts ever since.

Does he have a death wish, or does he simply not experience fear? Neither. In fact, big waves totally freak Pierce out. He says, "Pretty much everyone out there in those giant waves feels scared in one way or another. *They just surf anyway.*"

But, why?

The Greatest Threat

In order to understand why Andy Pierce does what he does, we first have to understand a few things about the nature of fear.

Our greatest threat as it relates to pursuing our goals isn't lack of time. It's not lack of education or lack of contacts or lack of qualification. It's not logistical challenges or even the doubt and criticism of others. Nope, the biggest threat we face is the fear we generate as we think about all these things. More specifically, our biggest threat is our inability to *overcome* that fear. Let me say that again: It's not the circumstances that we should feel threatened by, it's the *fear* of the circumstances that poses the real threat.

This is because unresolved fear cripples achievement. We want to achieve, but because of our fears, we are unable to. Fear causes us to exercise bad judgment and to make decisions from an emotional, unreliable, and downright unhealthy state of mind—all significant roadblocks on our way to success.

> **It's not the circumstances that we should feel threatened by, it's the fear of the circumstances that poses the real threat.**

Another very real threat posed by fear is that if it is not properly mitigated and overcome, it can be absolutely debilitating. Ultimately, that's why so many people stay stuck. They're so afraid of making the wrong choice, heading in the wrong direction, or looking stupid, that they don't ever go anywhere at all.

The bottom line is that people with high aspirations are going to experience a proportionately high level of fear. Renowned Harvard professor Chris Argyris said, "Behind this high aspiration for success is an equally high fear of failure." Essentially, fear is the freaky troll under the bridge that leads to achievement, and there's no way around, only through. If you choose not to manage your fear, in whatever form it takes for you individually, eventually your choice will equate to zero goal achievement.

Here's the real kicker: If high aspirations are equal to high fear, then the flip side to that truth is that overcoming high fear is equal to achieving high aspirations. Learning how to effectively manage and work through fear is a high-performance skill that leads to achieving goals.

HIGH ASPIRATIONS = HIGH FEAR

FEAR MANAGEMENT = PERFORMANCE

PERFORMANCE = GOAL ACHIEVEMENT

> **HIGH ASPIRATIONS = HIGH FEAR**
>
> **FEAR AVOIDANCE = PERFORMANCE AVOIDANCE**
>
> **PERFORMANCE AVOIDANCE = ZERO GOAL ACHIEVEMENT**

Defining Why

Why would someone do something they're afraid of?

Well, let's refer back to the story of Andy Pierce. Remember his comment? He said, "Pretty much everyone out there in those giant waves feels scared in one way or another. *They just surf anyway.*"

But *why?*

The question lends the answer: why.

When Pierce catches big waves, he's reaching his high aspirations. The joy he feels when he's doing what he loves is his *why*. For him, the feeling of being in the water, chasing the big swells, is absolutely worth overcoming his fear.

Pierce is doing what others only dream about.

What is your personal *why?* Defining the reasons you're working toward your high aspirations is the first and greatest way to work toward overcoming debilitating fears. You may be able to squeak by for a short time on will alone, but when the going gets tough, when the waves start to crash, and when fear begins to rear its ugly

> People successfully overcome fear
> when the "why" behind what they're afraid
> of is bigger than the fear itself.

head, you're in for a rude awakening if you don't have an equally powerful *why* to which you're solidly connected.

> High goals require equally high purpose.
> High purpose is your *why*.
> Your *why* helps you choose to act in the face of fear.

Why you do what you do creates the hope and determination necessary to make the choice to *act* in the face of fear.

The Fear Compensation Model: Overcoming Fear with Small Wins

Andy Pierce didn't go out and challenge a twenty-foot wave his first time in the ocean. Over many, many years, Pierce learned to surf on smaller waves, and he experienced many, many smaller spills. From small-wave success and failure, he learned how to *incrementally tolerate* greater and greater big-wave fear—from small shore break, to head-high waves, to twelve-foot waves, to twenty-foot waves and so on. And even when he "failed," so to speak, from a literally crushing experience, there was no question in his mind as to whether or not he'd get back in the water, because his *why* was stronger than his fear.

> "Decide that you want it more than you are afraid of it."
> —BILL COSBY

Let me introduce you to what I call the Fear Compensation Model. I call it that for two reasons. First, you have to *compensate* for the fear. You must counterbalance the fear with something else—you must do something to make up for your fear. And second, fear, when dealt with effectively, compensates you; it pays in dividends of success.

As aspirations rise, fears rise in equal measure along the performance line leading toward your goal. At the ultimate low point on the Fear Compensation Model, you have zero aspirations. This is absolute apathy. You have zero fears and zero action. What's there to worry about? What's there to do? You don't care about anything whether it's good or bad.

However, no one is absolutely apathetic. As your needs, wants, and goals grow in your mind, so do your fears. You start to think of all the obstacles that make the process of starting seem less and less attractive. You begin

The Fear Compensation Model: As aspirations rise, fears rise in equal measure along the performance line leading toward your goal.

to feel overwhelmed. The temptation then is to practice fear avoidance (whether consciously or subconsciously), and once you do that, you'll fail to perform and thus fail to reach your goals.

So how do you move up the line from zero—the starting point, where you're sitting on the ground level, looking up at your high hopes, high dreams, and equally high fears—to the finish point, where you've overcome obstacles, including (especially) fear, and reached your big goals and aspirations?

Get *small wins.*

Small wins, a term coined by psychologist Karl Weick, are the way we compensate for our fears and make sure we don't fall into fear-based inactivity. Begin by targeting

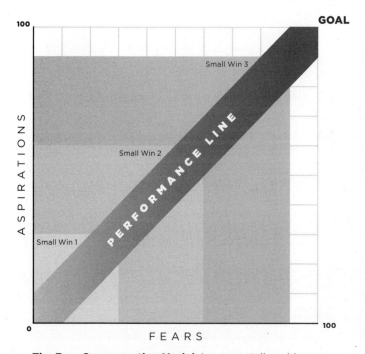

The Fear Compensation Model: Incrementally achieve one *small win* atop the other along the performance line to compensate for fear and reach your goal.

small goals and overcoming small fears that lead toward your ultimate goal. Trying to make a single leap from zero to one hundred along the performance line is absurd. That's like trying to surf twenty-foot Hawaiian waves when you don't yet know how to swim. Instead, make incremental leaps that are in direct alignment with your goals.

The Fear Compensation Model: Through small-wave success and failure, you can learn how to incrementally tolerate greater and greater big-wave fear.

> *"To recast larger problems into smaller, less arousing problems, people can identify a series of controllable opportunities of modest size that produce visible results."*
>
> —KARL WEICK, PSYCHOLOGIST WHO COINED THE TERM "SMALL WINS"

With each fear you overcome, from one small win to the next, you move farther and farther up the performance line. Each incrementally higher fear becomes progressively more tolerable, because you're developing the skills necessary to overcome your fears. To crush fear doesn't mean you eliminate it; crushing fear means you literally crush it down into smaller, more manageable parts and tackle one piece at a time.

> *"Don't be afraid to give your best to what seemingly are small jobs. Every time you conquer one it makes you that much stronger. If you do the little jobs well, the big ones will tend to take care of themselves."*
>
> —DALE CARNEGIE

What Happens When You Fail?

As illustrated in the Fear Compensation Model, as aspirations rise, so do fears. Thus, as goals rise, so must purpose. When each incremental fear is overcome, your confidence will grow, and this increased confidence serves to further solidify your sense of purpose—your connection to your personal *why*.

> Overcoming fear is a conscious decision
> you must make in order to start your "stupid" idea
> and move toward living a truly purposeful life.

The remarkable flip side to this principle is that failure *also* serves to solidify your connection to your personal why. Every time you fail, you are forced to reevaluate your overarching why, and every time you are forced to go back to the ultimate why behind your project, your connection to it grows stronger. Over time, through small wins, and through failure and success alike, you can keep progressing, even when you fail, because your commitment to your why has grown so much bigger than your fear.

*"There is only one thing
that makes a dream impossible to
achieve: the fear of failure."*

—PAULO COELHO, AUTHOR OF *THE ALCHEMIST*

WHATEVER IT TAKES.

9

End Pride:
The Humble Power Alternative

"Pride costs more than hunger, thirst, and cold."
—THOMAS JEFFERSON

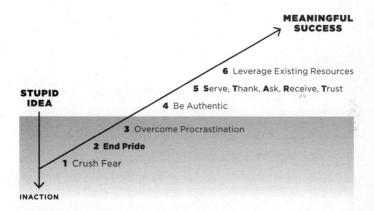

At the time of my son's death, I felt I was on a "smart" path toward "success." I was president of a financial services company in Hawaii and dabbled in real estate and small business development consulting in my spare time. Life was good. I set my own hours and made time for my family. *In theory,* all this flexibility left me plenty of discretionary time to pursue hobbies and interests as well as work toward other life goals. I had intentionally set up my life to allow me the freedom to do what I wanted to do and be where I wanted to be 24/7. I was living all of my dreams . . . except that I wasn't.

Despite the flexibility my life provided, this was my reality: I wasn't doing what I loved. I wasn't leaning into and returning to stupid like I knew I should. I wasn't actively pursuing the ideas that were constantly pressing on my mind. My dream of becoming an author was on the back burner, and while I was speaking and presenting (both passions of mine) for the financial services company, frankly, it just wasn't material that I was extraordinarily passionate about. I'd been lulled into a sense of security by my *comfortable* life.

So, despite the lack of sincere passion for my daily pursuits and despite the lack of connection to my dreams, I had convinced myself that my life was good, and it was . . . good *enough*.

To say the bottom fell out of my life after my son died would be a gross understatement. There is nothing like the death of someone you love to strip away the frivolities of life and magnify those things that are vitally important. When your entire life is suddenly staring you down, and you realize how very little of it makes any real sense, starting something stupid is suddenly the very smartest (and the only) thing you want to do.

I wasn't going to sit around and wait to see what the next weeks and months would bring. Our family had experienced a huge tragedy that shook us (especially our little ones) to the core—nothing mattered more than that. So, I did the stupid thing, and I resigned from my position as president of the financial services company. Natalie and I dropped everything and took our boys on a three-month traveling and healing adventure. We logged thousands of miles traveling back and forth across the United States; we even traveled internationally. We intentionally traveled by car with no DVD player and no video games to keep the kids occupied—it was just me, my wife, our kids, nature, and the open road.

We traveled from Honolulu, Hawaii, to Orlando, Florida, to Seattle, Washington, up to Calgary, Canada, and down to San Diego, California: camping, hiking, biking, fishing, playing guitar, laughing, crying, and making wonderful memories all along the way. I even squeezed in a personal trip with one of my best friends to surf in Costa Rica—fulfilling a lifelong, long-forgotten, dream of mine.

When we returned home, I stopped pursuing any project that wasn't directly aligned with the overarching goals of my life. I spent the next few years focused only on the things that mattered the most to me (including finishing this book). It wasn't an easy decision to make—people thought I was out of my mind, or completely bereft (or likely, both). Letting go of nearly every part of my former life required me to relinquish every ounce of my pride, and truthfully, it wasn't an easy decision to remain committed to my plan when the going got rough. Yes, embracing the New Smart took a large dose of humility and a *lot* of courage (for both Natalie and me). However, as I faced the fears associated with actually making the leap and actively pursuing *meaningful success*—on my own terms—I entered what has proven to be the most deeply satisfying, and successful, era of my life so far.

> *"Remembering that I'll be dead soon is the most important tool I've ever encountered to help me make the big choices in life. Because almost everything—all external expectations, all pride, all fear of embarrassment or failure—these things just fall away in the face of death, leaving only what is truly important."*
> —STEVE JOBS

The Destructive Nature of Pride

Why do so many people, businesses, marriages, and even entire empires fall? We've probably heard the proverb "Pride goeth before a fall" but could the answer really be that simple? Arguably, all other vices could fall under the umbrella called pride, and if pride really is at the heart of humanity's greatest ills, then it is, by that measure, the most destructive power in the world.

Obviously we're not talking about the kind of pride a mother feels for her child, or the pride you feel for your country, or the pride you experience when your team wins a big game. We're discussing the kind of pride that keeps people blinded, stuck, and isolated. The kind of pride that prevents them from experiencing lasting success.

People have trouble reaching goals and pursuing dreams for one (or many) of the following pride-related reasons:

- They are too prideful to risk appearing stupid.
- Pride convinces them that they've already done enough—they experience a sense of entitlement.
- Their pride causes them to blame others (or their circumstances) for their lack of success.
- Prideful people buy into a scarcity mentality—"In order for me to succeed, you must fail."

These are a handful of ways pride keeps people stuck where they are. But stupid people know that doing the crazy thing—even if that means being humble enough to drop everything and begin again—is a winning formula for success.

How to End Pride

1. Embrace Vulnerability:
Don't Be Scared of Looking Stupid

The line between fear and pride is nearly imperceptible. At the heart of pride, is the fear of looking stupid. Pride convinces people to feel justified in quitting because, for prideful people, approval is sought at all costs—even at the cost of success.

When pride shows up as the fear of looking stupid, it is the polar opposite of the New Smart. Here are some examples:

- If the New Smart is innovative, pride is rigid and unyielding.
- If the New Smart is unconventional, pride is unwilling to disrupt the status quo.
- If the New Smart is leaning into fear, pride is being controlled by fear.
- If the New Smart is turning down the volume on critics, pride is allowing the opinions of others to overpower you.
- If the New Smart is trusting the voice inside your own head, pride is seeking approval at the sacrifice of your own dreams.

Prideful people like to appear as if they have everything figured out. They are terrified of being wrong or, worse, they are afraid of appearing *vulnerable*. These fears put them on very dangerous ground, because people who have been captured by this category of pride won't ask for help, they won't ask questions, and they don't want to do anything to challenge the status quo.

> *"When we experience pride, we want to maintain the status quo. We are unwilling to change or move."*
>
> —HALE DWOSKIN, AUTHOR OF *THE SEDONA METHOD*

To overcome this type of pride, one must understand that vulnerability is a *good* thing. It inspires us to seek continual learning, and, most important, it grants us the courage to *change*. Brené Brown, research professor at the University of Houston Graduate College of Social Work, says, "Vulnerability is not weakness. . . . [It's] emotional risk, exposure, uncertainty. It fuels our daily lives. . . . Vulnerability is our most accurate measurement of courage." Brown continues, "Vulnerability is the birthplace of *innovation, creativity* and *change*"—all components of the New Smart.

Overcome the pride born from fear of looking stupid by embracing vulnerability.

2. Remember: Work Pays in Dividends of Success

Pride causes people to experience feelings of entitlement. They expect maximum results from minimal effort and throw their hands up in the air when things don't immediately go their way. Well, news flash: the world owes you nothing. This is a hard reality to swallow in a world plagued by patterns of entitlement.

> *"He who would accomplish little must sacrifice little. He who would achieve much must sacrifice much. He who would attain highly must sacrifice greatly."*
>
> —JAMES ALLEN, AUTHOR OF *AS A MAN THINKETH*

No amount of effort spent today will excuse us from the necessary work of tomorrow. Don't get me wrong, I'm all for working smart and maximizing effectiveness and efficiency. There is danger, however, in feelings of entitlement that lead to whining or self-pity when efforts seem to go unnoticed and/or don't lead to immediate results. I love this quote from Thomas Jefferson, "I'm a great believer in luck, and I find the harder I work, the more I have of it."

Have you ever had a lazy coworker? Or spent any amount of time around someone whose favorite hobby was complaining about how the universe was out to get them? It's horrible—there's no better description than that. People who let pride drag them down to that type of thinking or behavior are guaranteed to lose friends and opportunity in the process.

On the other hand, have you ever had a coworker who had an amazing work ethic? Or spent a significant amount of time with a person who was upbeat, grateful, and optimistic? These types of people are refreshing to be around. In fact, it's hard to wish anything but the very best for these types of people. It's easy to find yourself invested in their success and eager and willing to help them along the way. This is the kind of behavior you want to embody. You'll gain friends, mentors, and opportunity along the way.

Combat prideful feelings of entitlement by rolling up your sleeves, expressing gratitude and cheerfully getting to work.

3. Take Responsibility for Your Life: Don't Blame Others

When my wife was a little girl, her mother had little tolerance for reactive behavior. My wife recalls,

> I have a memory of grocery shopping with my mom when I was around six years old. I wanted my mom to purchase a certain brand of sugary cereal. The odds of a favorable response were not on my side. Those kinds of cereals weren't allowed in our

home aside from special occasions such as birthdays or camping trips. When she told me no, I responded by starting to cry. I don't remember the details of my behavior, but I know I was acting very irrationally, even for a six-year-old. I eventually wrapped up my tantrum monolog—which likely included all the reasons she was destroying my life by denying me bowlfuls of refined sugar for breakfast—and my mom was just *standing there*. She was calm and completely unaffected. If she had been embarrassed by my behavior, she certainly didn't show it. In a last-ditch effort to get a rise out of her, I wailed, "Mom! You make me sooooooo maaaaaad!" and as calm as can be, my mother gently responded, "Wait a minute, who makes Natalie mad when she's mad?"

Of all the lessons my amazing mother has taught me throughout my life, this is the one I am most grateful for. That day in the supermarket, she taught me that I am never absolved of responsibility for my own behavior. No matter what happens, I am always in charge of me.

The art of ownership is a dying one. Everyone wants to point the finger somewhere else. Pride that comes from blame is dangerous, because it causes people to feel *justified* in their inaction. After all, it's not their fault, because nothing ever is. Here are a few examples:

- "My marriage is failing because my parents were divorced. I never learned what it takes to make a marriage work."
- "I can't move up in my company because my boss doesn't like me. He's a jerk."
- "She got the raise instead of me because she is a suck-up."
- "He's successful because his parents were rich. I'm a failure because mine were poor."
- "People like her because she's cool and pretty. I'm all alone because I'm not."

In each of the previous scenarios we see how blame enables people to feel justified in staying trapped where they are. In these vignettes, people allow their circumstances to keep them stuck where they are rather than take ownership of the things they can control and move forward.

If you've experienced a real tragedy in your past, I'm *genuinely* sorry. But remember, you didn't *suffer* a tragedy, you *triumphed* over one. You can now make the choice to turn that triumph into even greater triumphs as your life moves forward. Staying in the past is blessing no one. It only makes you miserable and, worst of all, it completely suffocates your potential.

You can begin to break free of this kind of pride, by

always taking ownership of yourself. In the book *Good to Great,* legendary business consultant Jim Collins uncovered what it takes for a company to be great. After five years of colossal research, Collins and his team of researchers found something unexpected.

The data overwhelmingly concluded that the greatest companies had what Collins called "Level 5 leadership." He related that such leaders "embody a paradoxical mix of personal humility and professional will." According to Collins, "Level 5 leaders look out the window to attribute success to factors other than themselves. When things go poorly, however, they look in the mirror and blame themselves, taking full responsibility." On the other hand, the less successful companies had leaders who "often did just the opposite—they looked in the mirror to take credit for success, but out the window to assign blame for disappointing results."

Overcome blame and prideful excuses by taking ownership of your life.

4. Embrace Abundance: Don't Validate Your Success by the Failure of Others

Pride often manifests itself in an insatiable desire to be the *very* best, no matter the cost. People who have fallen victim to this kind of pride measure the validity of their own success by how much more successful they are than others.

Do you ever put others down to build yourself up?

Do you feel justified in stepping on others to get to the top?

Do you ever feel secretly (or openly) excited when someone else fails?

Do you ever feel secretly (or openly) jealous when someone else succeeds?

These kinds of feelings and behaviors are indicative of scarcity thinking, and this school of thought ultimately stems from pride. Scarcity thinking says, "There's not enough to go around" and "opportunities are few and far between."

Imagine we are sitting together on a bench in the park, and I say to you, "Stop breathing, right now, or there will not be enough air for me." Scarcity thinking is equally absurd. The ruthless need for success that comes from this type of pride is blinding. It causes us to approach things like love, happiness, and success as consumable resources—"The more these blessings are received by other people, the less there will be leftover for me."

Stephen R. Covey said it best:

> [People with a scarcity mentality] see life as having only so much. . . . [They] have a very difficult time sharing recognition and credit, power or profit. . . . They also have a hard time being genuinely happy for the success of other people. The Abundance Mentality, on the other hand, flows out of a deep inner sense of personal worth and security. It is the paradigm that there is plenty out there and enough to spare for everybody. It results in sharing of prestige, of recognition, of profits, of decision making. It opens possibilities, options, alternatives, and creativity.

Abundance thinking is embodied completely by the New Smart. When we consciously apply ourselves to abundant thinking, "It opens possibilities, options, alternatives, and creativity"—all pseudonyms for the New Smart!

We can overcome pride when we view the world from a perspective of abundance, and we simultaneously (and instantaneously) experience more genuine peace and fulfillment in our lives. We are also more accessible to success, because we become collaborative rather than divisive, thus opening ourselves up to the New Smart and the world of possibilities it brings.

Overcome the prideful need to measure your worth by how much more successful you are than

others, by operating from a core belief grounded in abundance.

Avoid Pride Creep: Embrace the Humble Power Alternative

It's common to blur the line between pride and confidence, and it's just as common for people to confuse humility with weakness. These misconceptions must end here, or the potential for highest possible achievement will unavoidably falter.

There is power born of humility. Drawing again from *Good to Great,* Collins asserts that great leaders "are resolved to do whatever it takes to make the company great, no matter how big or hard the decisions." In essence, Collins suggests that high-achieving leaders have the ability to seek the greatest good of the company— without letting personal agenda or personal pride get in the way. This is humility, and in this context, there's absolutely *nothing* weak about it. Humility, when embodied in this way, demonstrates insightfulness, courage, self-control, and integrity. Humility, in business and in life, is a powerful asset and does not denote lowliness, unimportance, or self-deprecation.

In fact, authentic self-confidence should be sought after and diligently increased. Authentic confidence in our ability to perform is essential to attaining our highest potential achievements. In these ways, self-confidence clearly differs from pride. If someone has significant confidence in their ability to perform, that person is not necessarily full of pride.

An enlightened understanding of ego is essential to fully appreciate the importance of self-confidence in peak performance and success. For most, the word "ego" has an immediately negative connotation. In the compelling book, *Egonomics,* authors David Marcum and Steven Smith discuss the ironic "dual nature" of ego, stating, "it is both a valuable asset, and a deep liability." The authors assert, "In the right amount, ego is inherently positive and provides a healthy level of confidence and ambition—driving out insecurity, fear, and apathy." The danger comes when ego is "left unchecked."

When ego is kept within the healthy bounds of humility, it lends itself to high performance—in the form of qualities such as self-confidence, innovation, and courage (all components of the New Smart). When ego abandons humility and gives way to pride, however, it can turn our greatest strengths into our most damaging weaknesses—"self-confident" becomes "self-absorbed," "innovative" becomes "impractical," and "courage" becomes "reckless."

The phenomenon we observe when ego is left unchecked and gives way to pride, is what I call *pride creep.*

Pride creep is detrimental to high-potential success and must be avoided at all costs. We free ourselves from the damaging effects of pride creep when we embrace the *Humble Power Alternative*. This powerful alternative is achieved by working to keep our egos in check.

To employ the Humble Power Alternative:

- Instead of being too prideful to risk appearing stupid, courageously lean into the New Smart.
- Instead of insisting that what you've already done is enough, do more.
- Instead of blaming others for your lack of success, take ownership.
- Instead of hoping others will fail, encourage their success.

Practice the Humble Power Alternative and achieve greater satisfaction and success in all aspects of business and life.

CLEAR THE CLUTTER MAKE ROOM FOR YOUR DREAMS

10

Overcome Procrastination:
Breaking the "Tomorrow" Habit

"My own behavior baffles me. For I find myself doing what I really loathe but not doing what I really want to do."
—St. Paul

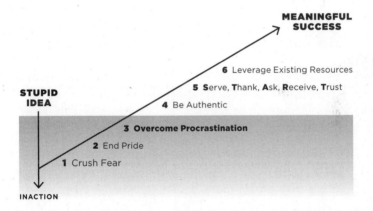

I once attended a business training meeting in Honolulu with a CEO from out of town. After the training concluded, my wife and I were invited to accompany this man, his family, and a small group of friends on a chartered boat the following day. I was honored by the invitation and, admittedly, I was also excited for the wonderful opportunity it would be to get to know this man on a personal level.

We lived about an hour from the harbor, but we planned to leave our home especially early to ensure that we would arrive on time. The following morning, however, I got caught up in other things, and our departure time kept getting pushed later and later as I rushed to complete these "important" tasks. Ironically, I can't even remember what it was I was working on at the time, but what I do remember, what I will *never* forget, is standing on the dock with my wife, watching the boat coast around the point and out of view.

I had procrastinated, and I had—literally—missed the boat.

Procrastination threatens to rob us of those things that are most important in our lives. As the saying goes, "Time waits for no man." In short, when we procrastinate, we risk missing the boat.

Why We Procrastinate

Question: How long does it take a Nobel Prize–winning economist to mail a box?
Answer: Eight months.

George Akerlof, Nobel Prize–winning economist, wrote of an experience he had:

> Some years back, when I was living in India for a year, a good friend of mine, Joseph Stiglitz, visited me; because of unexpected limitations on carry-on luggage at the time of his departure, he left with me a box of clothes to be sent to him in the United States. Both because of the slowness of transactions and my own ineptitude in such matters, I estimated that sending this parcel would take a full day's work. Each morning for over eight months I woke up and decided that the next morning would be the day to send the Stiglitz box. This occurred until a few months before my departure when I decided to include it in the large shipment of another friend who was returning to the United States at the same time as myself.

After reflecting on this incident, Akerlof found he "did not have rational expectations" in putting off sending the box.

I share this story for two reasons. The first, and more obvious reason, is to shed light on the irrational thought process we engage in when we procrastinate. Consistent irrational decision-making—saying you'll do it tomorrow, then not doing so and adding yet another day to complete the task—is similar to the irrational decision-making process many people use when bound by an addiction. Akerlof says, "Most drug abusers, like most chronically overweight individuals, fully intend to cut down their intake, since they recognize that the long-run cost of their addiction exceeds its benefits. They intend to stop—tomorrow."

We are likewise aware that "the long-run cost" of procrastinating our inspired ideas "exceeds its benefits." Yet, we procrastinate anyway. This illogical behavior is preventing us from living our best life.

The second, more subtle, yet equally important reason I share this story is to demonstrate that no one is outside procrastination's reach. Procrastinators tend to believe themselves lazy and incapable. They are thus plagued by feelings of weakness and even worthlessness, yet when we understand that procrastination happens to the best of us—even Nobel Prize–winning economists— we can more easily shake discouragement and find the power to overcome this destructive habit.

Two Myths of Procrastination

Myth One: Procrastinators are lazy.
Reality: Procrastinators can be workaholics.

Mike Michalowicz, a successful entrepreneur and author, was proud of his twelve-hour workdays and his eighty-hour workweeks. But when he reduced his work-day to nine to five, he discovered something interesting about himself. He said, "Ironically, when I forced my-self to leave work each day by 5 P.M., my whole sched-ule changed. I started skipping the nonsense distrac-tions, such as the constant checking of e-mail, or surfing (ahem—researching) the Internet. I actually got down to work during that time. My per-hour productivity skyrock-eted! And I was getting more done in a 9-to-5 day than I used to in an entire 'workaholic day.'"

Jason Fried and David Heinemeier Hansson, au-thors of the book *Rework,* say, "In the end, workahol-ics don't actually accomplish more than nonworkaholics. They may claim to be perfectionists, but that just means they're wasting time fixating on inconsequential details instead of moving on to the next task. Workaholics aren't heroes. They don't save the day, they just use it up. The real hero is already home because she figured out a faster way to get things done."

Myth Two: Procrastinators live in the future.
Reality: "Procrastinators live in the now."

Procrastinators are addicted to immediacy, and that makes it difficult to engage in tasks that don't produce the satisfaction of immediate results. It is this addiction to immediacy that makes them prone to impulsiveness and thus procrastination. In fact, Piers Steel, author of *The Procrastination Equation,* states that "scores of studies based on many thousands of people have established that impulsiveness . . . shares the strongest bond with procrastination." Thus, ironically, procrastinators actually live in the now.

When we procrastinate, we fill our lives with the tasks that are right in front of us rather than make the concerted effort to leave enough room in our schedules to pursue dreams. Procrastination is like going to a fancy restaurant and filling up on bread and not leaving enough room for dinner.

John Perry, a professor of philosophy, describes procrastination in this way:

> Procrastinators seldom do absolutely nothing; they do marginally useful things, like gardening or sharpening pencils or making a diagram of how they will reorganize their files when they get around to it. Why does the procrastinator do these things? Because they are a way of not doing something more important. If all the procrastinator had left to do was to sharpen some pencils, no force on earth could get him [to] do it.
>
> However, the procrastinator can be motivated to do difficult, timely and important tasks, as long as

these tasks are a way of not doing something more important.

Don't get me wrong, living in the now is a good thing. The lesson here is to live in the now by engaging in the most *important* activities today (dream work). When we live in the now and perpetually push what is most important to tomorrow by filling our time with less important activities, procrastination is robbing us of the most significant and fulfilling opportunities of our lives.

Understanding Procrastination

Drawing from multiple sources such as dictionary definitions, Latin roots of the word, studies of vocational behavior, and academic journals, here is my definition of procrastination: *Procrastination is the counterproductive act of choosing to postpone doing something important until a later time.*

For perpetual procrastinators, understanding procrastination is akin to understanding ourselves. When we understand what is really happening when we procrastinate, we are better able to understand the cause(s) behind our own tendency to procrastinate. And when we understand why we procrastinate—on an individual level—we are better equipped to formulate a reasonable defense. I'll illustrate with an example from my own experience.

I struggle with procrastination, particularly when it comes to writing (to which my wonderful editor, Lisa, will gladly attest). I share the lament one Master's candidate included in his final thesis on the subject of procrastination: "When it is hard to find the right words, it is easier to play a game instead." Boy, do I relate.

At times, I find writing to be completely arduous. I find myself doing laundry, washing dishes, running errands, and poking myself with a fork in order to escape the task of writing. Admittedly, I also find myself choosing my favorite small luxuries like eating out, surfing, playing guitar, and going on family outings over writing. The ironic revelation is that, despite the inherent difficulties I face when writing, the truth is that I actually *want* to write! Further, I actually *like* to write! Yet I procrastinate anyway. I echo the words of St. Paul, "My own behavior baffles me. For I find myself doing what I really loathe but not doing what I really want to do." While the tasks I choose instead of writing are often productive, refreshing, and may even complete other tasks on my to-do list, they are keeping me from doing the things that are most important to me. No matter why or how I choose to procrastinate, it is no question that procrastination gets in my way.

In pondering this personal paradox, I have been enlightened by the discovery that when writing feels hard, or when I feel overwhelmed by related tasks such as researching and compiling data, procrastination steps in as a compelling distraction. I now see this tendency for what it is and consciously work to avoid it.

Are You Procrastinating?

Most people who procrastinate are glaringly aware that they are neglecting what is most important to them by filling their time with less important things. However, it is common for people to be neck deep in patterns of procrastination without even recognizing it. This happens when people genuinely believe that they are unable to act on their most important goals because of time-related restraints. They say, "I can't do this important thing—the thing I'd *most* like to accomplish—right now because these other important obligations take up all my time." Remember, procrastination doesn't always come in the form of frivolous activities. Often we're filling our time with good or even *essential* tasks, but even so, anytime you postpone doing the things that are most important in your life, you are falling victim to procrastination.

No matter the reason behind our procrastination, the result is the same: "Procrastination is the grave in which opportunity is buried" (the slogan of Procrastinators

Anonymous). Procrastination must be overcome or it will rob you of the things that could be most significant in your life.

Overcoming Procrastination

The following are some steps to help us overcome procrastination.

Step 1: Make Time

We must consciously set aside time to work toward our most important goals. According to Parkinson's Law, "Work expands so as to fill the time available for its completion." By this measure, if we do not make time for the things that matter most, the other less important tasks of the day will inevitably seep into every minute available to us, leaving no time leftover for the most meaningful pursuits in our lives.

> *"You must never find time for anything, if you want time you must make it."*
> —CHARLES BUXTON, BRITISH SOCIAL REFORMER AND PHILANTHROPIST

Step 2: Simplify

Overcoming procrastination is not, I repeat, *not* about cramming additional work into your day—that would be unsustainable over the long haul toward success. Rather, overcoming procrastination is about simplifying your life to make space for the activities that matter most.

The famous artist Hans Hoffman once said, "The ability to simplify means to eliminate the unnecessary so that the necessary may speak." Likewise, the ability to overcome procrastination requires eliminating the unnecessary tasks in your life so that there is room to engage in what is most necessary to achieving your high-potential goals.

> *"Things which matter most must never be at the mercy of things which matter least."*
> —JOHANN WOLFGANG VON GOETHE

Take inventory of the way you regularly spend your time. One way to do this effectively is to track the time you spend *not* working on your projects. For example, if the Internet is a constant time-killer for you, set a timer to track how long you're spending online. This exercise will be a real eye-opener for many.

I like to set an alarm to ring every fifteen minutes in order to keep myself on task. When the alarm goes off, it reminds me to check in with myself to see if I'm being productive or if I'm wasting time. Once I get in the zone, I turn off the alarm and simply focus on the work at hand.

The ultimate goal is to weed out nonessential tasks. Please note that this doesn't mean eliminating all leisure activity from your life. Participating in activities you enjoy refuels you. Such activities provide a respite from the taxing nature of hard work and are essential to maintaining a sustainable pace toward your goals. Simplifying your life also doesn't mean that you must cut out everything but work from your schedule in order to avoid falling victim to procrastination. Simplifying means you consciously "clear the clutter" in order to make room for the things that matter most.

Steps 3 through 6 are what I call the *Four Ps of Overcoming Procrastination* in starting your stupid idea: Make your idea *Public, Planned, Pleasurable,* and *Painful.*

Step 3: Make Your Stupid Idea Public

Tell someone else what you're trying to do. There is great power in the right kind of accountability.

Effective accountability is achieved in different ways for different people. Some find power in sharing their plans through Twitter, Facebook, blogs, and the like. These individuals are inspired by the amount of gravity a large and very public accountability group provides. On the other hand, it can be equally effective to simply tell a trusted friend.

The key is to find people to whom *you feel accountable.* Notice that I did not say *someone you know will hold you accountable.* If there is a person or group that you'd feel deep regret facing after breaking a promise, that is the perfect form of accountability for you. It is infinitely more effective than someone who is simply willing to crack the whip in your behalf.

Step 4: Plan Your Stupid Idea

Dreams don't get done until they're due. It is easy to find time to do everything else, except follow our dreams. This is because other important things in our lives have due dates—bills are due, assignments are due, even babies are due. If your dreams are never due, they'll never get done.

To effectively overcome procrastination, create a specific performance plan for your goal.

- Break your overarching goal into smaller, more manageable ones. These smaller goals are what management gurus refer to as **"S.M.A.R.T."**:
    - **Specific:** Goals must clearly express the expectations required for successful completion.
    - **Measurable:** There should be a system in place to effectively measure progress.
    - **Attainable:** Goals must be realistic.
    - **Relevant:** Goals should be a significant step toward your ultimate end in mind.
    - **Time-bound**: Goals must be assigned a deadline.

- Set aside specific time to work toward your S.M.A.R.T. goals. It's not enough to simply say, "I'm going to work toward my goals for three hours this week." It is more effective to say, "Monday, Wednesday, and Friday, from 8 to 9 a.m., I will work on these specific steps."
- Engage your accountability team in your plan so that when due dates for specific tasks arrive, you will be required to openly report on your progress.

If followed effectively, this process will help you get stuff done.

Step 5: Make the Process Pleasurable

In order to stay on track and avoid falling back into procrastination, you've got to reward yourself along the way.

Pleasurable rewards must be things that are immediately available, such as going to the movies, spending time with people you enjoy, or eating at a favorite restaurant. Don't reward yourself with a vacation, for example, unless the vacation is happening immediately.

The pleasure doesn't have to be elaborate. For instance, if the Internet is a consistent portal to procrastination, but you can't live without it, tell yourself you can't log on to the Internet until you've completed a certain task. If you're a fitness buff, tell yourself you can't exercise until you get that task done—that'll get you moving.

Step 6: Make the Process Painful

Assign a negative consequence if you don't complete specific tasks on time. This consequence can be in the form of having to do something you don't want to do, or it can be losing a privilege or possession you really love. Either way, the negative consequence must be significant enough to be a compelling motivator.

You may want to consider joining a movement such as stickK.com; that is, if losing your hard-earned money is coercive enough to keep you committed. StickK.com is a revolutionary service designed to help people overcome procrastination and get stuff done. Essentially, you go to the website, set a goal, and then put some money on the line to incentivize you to achieve your goal. Users can even select a "referee" who will hold them accountable and gather a group of supporters to cheer them on.

As a way to further motivate their users, stickK .com also allows participants to donate money to an organization or a cause they hate if they fail. StickK.com cofounder Jordan Goldberg said, "A lot of people write in and say, 'You know what really motivated me? The thought of giving money to the George Bush library, or the Bill Clinton library,' depending on your political views."

At the time of this writing, the site boasts more than $11.5 million at stake, more than 171,000 commitments created, more than 300,000 workouts completed, and more than 2,500,000 cigarettes not smoked.

The Irony of Procrastination

The ironic thing about procrastination is that it is rarely fully enjoyable, because the time spent in procrastination is simultaneously time and energy spent in worry, anxiety, and regret over what you know you *should* be doing instead. Thus not only does procrastination keep us from achieving the greatest dreams of our lives, but when we procrastinate, our time is tainted and not as fulfilling as it otherwise could be. And that's no way to live.

No more tomorrows. Today's the day.

"If you really want to do something, no one can stop you. But if you really don't want to do something, no one can help you."

—James A. Owen, author and speaker

THERE IS POWER IN

AUTHENTICITY

11

Be Authentic:
The Power of Authenticity

"I want you to be everything that's you,
deep at the center of your being."
—CONFUCIUS

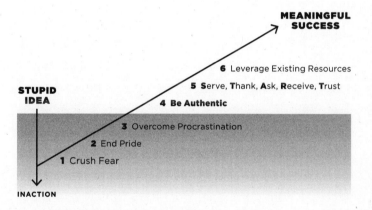

It was 1993, and Mike Colón had just graduated from high school. He sat down with his career counselor and was advised, "You should go into engineering. They're going to be hiring a lot of engineers." So, he did.

Colón enrolled at Cal State Fullerton, where he

began studying to become an engineer. But he was quickly bored. Engineering may have been a field where people were getting jobs, but Colón just didn't seem to fit. He wasn't in love. He recalled, "I definitely didn't have the same passion for engineering that the other students had."

At the time, Colón was working two part-time jobs: one as a waiter at Red Lobster and the other with a photography company that had been "willing to train whoever wants a job." He didn't know much about photography; he just took the job to pay the bills. But the more he shot, the better he got, and the better he got, the more he fell in love with photography. A year later, Colón quit his job at Red Lobster and was taking on additional photography jobs to put himself through school. It was 1997, and after four years of engineering with only one year to go before graduation, he decided he wanted to be a professional photographer.

"I just knew I couldn't be happy as an engineer," he recalled. "But even more than that, I knew how much I loved photography." So, he overcame his fears and dropped engineering. Since Cal State Fullerton didn't have a photography major, he switched to marketing instead, knowing it would help him build his photography business. Very few of his engineering credits transferred over, so Colón was essentially starting over from scratch.

That's right. He started over as a freshman again, with four more years of school ahead of him.

"I just couldn't let myself live a life I'd regret," he said. "I could have just stuck with it and finished my last year in engineering, but I knew that if I had that engineering degree, it would always be a temptation for me to choose money over happiness, especially when building my photography business got hard." When he weighed it out, Colón determined, "I would rather be poor doing something I authentically love, than rich doing something I don't."

Colón faced a lot of resistance for his decision. His parents were upset, and his girlfriend thought he was crazy (he ended up ending the relationship as a result), but these detractors were easy to ignore, because for the first time, college was *fun*. He was completely engaged with the content. He was going to school to learn about something that excited him, not just to do his time and earn a degree. He sat in front, asked the right questions, and met with professors after class. He says, "Everybody said I was stupid, but I had this strange sense of confidence. The kind of confidence that only comes when you know you're on the right track."

> *"I would rather be poor doing something I*
> *authentically love, than rich doing something*
> *I don't."*
>
> —MIKE COLÓN, PHOTOGRAPHER

Colón has gone on to achieve astonishing success as a professional wedding and lifestyle photographer. His portfolio boasts some of the biggest names in Hollywood, the music industry, and professional sports, including Usher, Timbaland, Hanna Gibson (Mel Gibson's daughter), and others. As a result of his stupid decision, he is now a spokesperson and sits on advisory boards for the industry's top corporations including Apple, Nikon, Epson, and more. When I asked Colón what advice he had for people who have crazy ideas, and detractors to overcome, he said,

> Whatever the risks are, you have to be willing to accept them 100 percent. You can't live in fear. You have to make the decision that even if your worst nightmares come true, it's still worth it to be doing what you love. Then get out there and make it work.

Success in Authenticity

As we develop a sense of our best possible self—and become authentic—we experience positive change. Authenticity and success go hand in hand. When Mike

Colón courageously gave up engineering to pursue photography, he was authentically choosing the most meaningful path for *him,* and this in turn led to meaningful success. Not only did his decision pay off financially, but more important, it paid off in dividends of increased energy, greater satisfaction and happiness, and a life truly free from regret.

In an interview with *TV Guide* about the final episode of *The Oprah Winfrey Show,* Oprah shared her secret to success: "The secret is authenticity. The reason people fail is because they're pretending to be something they're not." The kind of authentic success that Oprah is describing is about more than jumping ship and becoming a photographer, more than selling used jeans in Europe, and more even than learning to fly. While the stories in this book, and stupid ideas in general, are definitely sound examples of authentic life decisions, authenticity is much, much bigger than all that.

In some ways, the concept of "authenticity" is losing its core meaning as the term becomes more and more popularized. Authenticity carries so much significance to overall life fulfillment and success that it's important we take time to really "get it." We may say we just want to be authentic, and we may really mean it, but the reality is that culturally, we are becoming numbed to what authenticity really entails and the power it really has to affect positive change and high achievement in our lives.

Truly being authentic is knowing what matters to you, on the deepest level of who you are, and committing always to act from that authentic center. No matter the dream, no matter the goal, no matter the level of success you achieve, if your decisions are not aligned with the things in your life that matter very most, your success will be shallow and unfulfilling, to say the least. Until you act in ways that are aligned with who you authentically are, no matter how successful you become, there will always be an underlying and insatiable desire for more, more, more and an underlying hollowness in life. This is not real success.

Understanding Everything That's You

People love to say, "You gotta fake it till you make it." But this implies that the fake you is someone better than who you inherently are, and this is simply not the truth. Let me say this loud and clear: *The person you imagine yourself to be in the very best and most powerful moments of your life, is the* authentic *you.* And in truth, I imagine you're probably much more incredible even than that.

The great Chinese philosopher Confucius said, "I want you to be everything that's you, deep at the center of your being." Sounds amazing, right? So why is it so hard to consistently perform at that higher level? Why is it so hard to stay connected to the very best version of ourselves all the time? The problem isn't that we don't want to be authentic, nor is it that we don't buy into the fact that authenticity leads to more meaningful success. The truth is that most of us really do long to be everything that we really are. The real problem is that few of us know how to get to that place in our lives. Most of us simply don't know how to move from who we are *pretending to be* to who we truly are.

Operationalizing Authenticity

Every day, you either become more aligned with your authentic self or you move further away. And the difference lies completely in the choices you make. The following are five suggestions for how to make authenticity operational in your life.

1. Break Free of Fear, Pride, and Procrastination

When we act in ways that are not aligned with our highest potential, we move further and further away from who we authentically are. This leads to lack of fulfillment, lack of happiness, and an overall disconnect from what we really want for ourselves. Our life paradigm becomes clouded by external influences until we can no longer recognize our own inherent sense of direction or worth. For example:

- If we consistently act from a place of fear, we become governed by our fearful tendencies.
- If we consistently act from a place of pride, we become bound by its dangerous limitations.
- If we consistently act on impulse and procrastinate the most important things in our lives, we become trapped—constantly moving in circles. As if on an endless merry-go-round, we're always moving, never arriving anywhere good.

You can't become *who* you really are if you're living your life trapped inside an egg of fear, pride, or procrastination. Find courage in the words of James Allen, author of *As a Man Thinketh,* "You cannot travel within and stand still without." Break free from that shell, and you will come to know your true, authentic self. Until you do, the real you will never really be born.

> As you consciously break free from the self-imposed limitations in your life, you will find it incrementally easier to make the kinds of decisions that lead toward your highest personal potential. This is the key to discovering and unlocking your inherent self.

In other words, as you consistently act in ways that are aligned with what is truly most meaningful to you, over time, you will come to realize Confucius's great desire for all of mankind. You will come to know "everything that's you, deep at the center of your being."

2. "Find the Courage to Do Things You Are Not Ready to Do"

Marissa Mayer was one of the first twenty employees at Google and the first female engineer. She became the CEO of Yahoo! and is also the youngest woman, to date, to be included on the Forbes prestigious list of the "50 Most Powerful Women" in the world. When speaking at a commencement address at Illinois Institute of Technology, Mayer encouraged students to "find the courage to do things you are not ready to do." She said,

> Doing something you aren't ready to isn't comfortable. . . . But in pushing through that discomfort you learn a lot more about yourself. You learn to do something you didn't think you could do. Or you learn where your limits are. Either is valuable. It's important to push through that uneasiness though, because in that moment of finding your courage, you really grow and you really reach.

Stretch yourself and go outside your comfort zone. You'll often find that you're a lot stronger than you knew.

For example, I think middle school is the place self-worth goes to die, and I'm only partially kidding. When I was in seventh and eighth grade, I had very little confidence. I was a little shy, I felt awkward, and just about every interaction in my life made me feel uncomfortable. The change in my life came when I started to force myself to do things that I didn't feel ready to do—things that made me uncomfortable. I'm not talking about giving in to peer pressure or doing things that I knew were wrong. I'm referring to things that I knew were irrationally holding me back—like simply feeling good about myself and making sure my self-talk was positive.

Little by little, incrementally, these fears became easier and easier to overcome. Over time, I learned a lot about myself and became more and more self-confident. By the time I was in ninth grade, that shy, awkward kid wasn't totally gone, but I kept doing things that stretched me. I learned to play guitar, I formed a rock band, and I forced myself to get in front of people. Before I knew it, I found myself, mic in hand, playing in front of large crowds of people every weekend. (The shyness may have gone away, but I think I'll always be a little awkward!)

At first, as we attempt to make decisions that are aligned with our highest potential, there will be opportunities and choices that will require us to act in ways that might make us feel uncomfortable. One of the greatest opportunities we greet along the path toward greater authenticity is to become comfortable doing the uncomfortable. Every time we act anyway, in spite of fear and pride—in spite of discomfort—we will move closer to a more authentic, and thus genuinely successful, life.

3. Set Standards, Keep Them, and Get Respect

"The Quiksilver in Memory of Eddie Aikau is the most venerated big wave surfing event on Earth, held at Waimea Bay, Oahu, on a single day during the Hawaiian winter when, and if, waves exceed the 20-foot minimum requirement."

Only twenty-eight surfers (along with some alternates) are invited to compete, making this a very prestigious and coveted event. Because of these strict standards, "The Eddie"—as it's known—has only been held eight times over twenty-seven years (from 1984 through 2011)—"but those rare and special days are recognized as the most spectacular days in surfing history—for both surfers and spectators."

The surfing contest has no set date and is open between December 1 and the end of February in hopes the ocean will provide the right conditions. On January 21, 2011, the contest organizers gave the waves a "50/50 chance" that they'd be big enough the next day, and they spent the day preparing for the "world's most prestigious big wave event."

Thousands of people poured into Waimea Bay the next morning to watch and wait—not an easy thing when the parking lot has only fifty-five stalls. However, "after 4 hours of monitoring, only eight waves more than 20 feet had crashed Waimea Bay." Despite all the spectators, surfers, time, energy, and money that was put into the event, the contest was cancelled. The waves weren't "big enough for the namesake of the Quiksilver in Memory of Eddie Aikau."

How did the crowd react? One newspaper reported that they "actually clapped upon the announcement that there would be no contest on this day, apparently in respect of the process. Ever heard applause at a rainout?"

Quiksilver CEO Bob McKnight said this about the decision to cancel the contest:

> This event has created a life all its own and has come to stand for much more than just big wave riding.
>
> Standing on the beach at Waimea Bay on January 20, surrounded by tens of thousands of spectators from around the world, we were disappointed to have to call a No Go. But when the crowd began to cheer, we knew it was the right call and that The

Eddie represents something special that we all want to uphold.

Eddie was a young man of character, integrity and incredible athletic ability. His story took surfing's story across boundaries and around the world. Through his legacy, we look to inspire young generations of surfers for decades to come.

Standards were set. Standards were kept. And people respected that; they even applauded and cheered when they missed out on the event of a lifetime.

> *"The essence of being real, of acting with authenticity, is in knowing what you care about and then doing your best to be true to these values and aspirations."*
> —STEWART D. FRIEDMAN, AUTHOR

In order to truly live from our authentic core, we must always make decisions that are aligned with our authentic goals, and we must always be true to what we authentically believe.

Authenticity is based on the principle of integrity. If we are operating from a foundational commitment to authenticity, when we make a commitment, we keep it. But keeping commitments is only a surface-level description. Truly being authentic also means upholding personal standards when no one else is looking. As Gandhi taught, "To believe something and not to live it, is dishonest," and I would add, *even when no one else is watching.*

When authentic standards are kept, no matter the circumstances, we develop an enhanced ability to succeed. And two things happen:

- Our personal feelings of self-worth and confidence increase, and increased confidence leads to higher levels of competency.
- We earn the respect of others by gaining a reputation for consistency and integrity—which go hand in hand and serve as invaluable assets as we strive to attain our very highest aspirations.

4. Trust Yourself

If your goal is to be authentic, you need to understand your inherent worth. Even if your life has been a series of mistakes and failures, those are only things you *did;* they are not who you *are.* Do the work to make things right where necessary, forgive yourself, and move on. To paraphrase the words of author Paul Boese, forgiveness may not change your past, but it sure does enlarge your future.

Authentic people trust themselves, not in a prideful or self-centered way; rather they simply understand and appreciate their inherent worth. Authentic people have developed a sense of purpose in their lives and a real connection to what matters to them, and their connection to their self-worth serves as the foundation of their lives. As they consistently make decisions that are aligned with their authentic values and goals, their measure of their self-worth, and thus the strength of their foundation, increases. Grounded in self-worth, and achieved through genuine commitment to purpose, authenticity is a marvelous upward spiral toward meaningful success!

If you want to trust yourself, make decisions that are grounded in your authentic principles. Don't lie. Don't cheat. Don't push others down to obtain success. Those kind of behaviors are inauthentic and lead nowhere you'd ever want to be. Success that is obtained in any way that is not grounded in your genuine beliefs, goals, and values will never bring the authentic sense of fulfillment you seek.

Be good. Be happy. Be authentic. Achieve meaningful success.

5. Start Your Stupid Ideas

The simple process of getting clear about what it is you really want to do in your life, and then getting started, is one of the greatest practices in authenticity there is. So how do you get started?

- Exercise the courage to acknowledge your stupid ideas, despite doubt, fear, or the opinions of others.
- Start projects surrounding these ideas.
- Find your voice and uncover your authentic self.

> *"[Authentic people are] actively and intentionally pursuing a life in accord with their deepest potentials."*
> —MICHAEL KERNIS AND BRIAN GOLDMAN, AUTHORS

In other words, when you start on your stupid ideas, you kindle the fire of authenticity, giving the real you not only power, but *permission* to participate in your life!

Authentic Success: The Power of Being *You*

As you actively strive to live an authentic life, you will consistently be doing things that other people think are stupid. And that's okay. If you're truly committed to the kind of success and fulfillment that only authenticity can bring, sometimes you're going to have to do things that other people won't immediately understand. Remember, life is big, and there's no way under, over, or around it. You can only go through. You simply can't expect to be someone else through that process and still hope to live a truly meaningful life. If you want to be fulfilled, and live without regret, you have to be true to you—no matter the decisions or opinions of others.

When Mike Colón dropped engineering to pursue his passion for photography, people thought he was crazy. But the unexpected residual effect of his stupid decision was a heightened confidence in his own judgment. The *confidence* Mike gained when he decided to follow authentic meaning over money has fueled every personal and professional decision he has made from that point forward. "I consistently make decisions that other people call stupid," he says. "These types of choices are basically the foundation of my life."

One of the stupidest professional decisions Colón ever made happened only a few short years into his career. It was 2001, and digital photography was barely on the radar of the professional sector. Local photographers openly balked at its viability as a professional medium. "They were sighting reasons like lack of resolution, shadow detail, and overall image quality," Colón says, "but I think the underlying issue was that they didn't want to have to go out and buy new gear, mess with computers, or be forced to learn Photoshop."

No matter the overwhelming opinion of the industry, or the many practical (read: expensive) reasons he should stick with film, Colón still felt a strong urgency to make the switch. "More than ever, people told me I was crazy. They told me it was just a fad, and I was going to bankrupt myself before it had passed." Colón still made the leap and was the first one in the competitive Orange County professional circuit to go 100 percent digital. "The result was amazing," he recalls. "Being the early adopter got me noticed. Within months, I was the industry-wide expert on digital photography." He began speaking at workshops all over the country, photography magazines covered his story, and Nikon offered him a sponsorship and has been providing him with cutting-edge professional gear ever since.

"Within two short years of embracing the digital medium, everyone else had jumped on board, and here I was a veteran, the expert," Colón relates. "Trusting my authentic instinct and just going for it definitely paid off."

Around this same period of time when digital photography was becoming popular, another photographer, Jonathan Canlas, was facing a very different stupid decision. Canlas recalls, "Photographers left and right were making the switch [to digital], but I just couldn't do it." He loved the look and feel of film. It wasn't that he had a horrible opinion of digital photography; the issue was that film felt like an authentic extension of his art, and he couldn't give that up. "I attempted to switch," he remembers, "but every time I did, I realized it was just not *me*. I was no longer creating images for myself, I was just doing what everyone else was doing."

It's important to note that although Canlas was

refusing to adapt to the tide of the industry, he was not being maladaptive in the sense that qualifies his decision as unhealthy stupid. He was being authentic. He was trusting his stupid decision despite the overwhelming opinion of others. He knew that if he switched to digital, he would not be producing the kind of product he really wanted to produce.

As a result of his stupid decision, Canlas has taken the luxury wedding market by storm. "Film is not dead," he says. "It really is a thriving medium, no matter how niche it may be." His steady increase in business tells him he's right. It turns out that being one of the few photographers that still shoots exclusively in film has served to set him apart from his competition.

Canlas now finds himself traveling all over the world, teaching sold-out workshops on the medium that was once considered all but dead, and contributing to a major resurgence in film as a professional medium. He also earned a sponsorship from Kodak, and they now use his images worldwide to push their products. Canlas offers this advice to other entrepreneurs:

> In any field, you can't care about what the guy down the street is doing. You have to do what works for *you* and *your* business. . . . Blaze your own path. It is more scenic and rough all at once, but it ends up being the most rewarding. To be successful in

business, you have to offer something dynamic, and most dynamic products are not found along the beaten path.

I definitely had people telling me I was crazy or I'd be washed up if I did not jump on this wave. Well, that wave has come and gone. I stuck with what I wanted, and ironically, a lot of those people who said I'd be washed up, are [now out of business] and I'm at the top of my game.

The juxtaposition of these two stories powerfully illustrates the unequaled power of authenticity. When you make decisions from a *true* foundation of authenticity, no matter what those decisions are, not only are you more engaged and fulfilled in your life, but the likelihood of your success will increase. Ultimately, authenticity is less about *what you do,* and more about *why you do it.*

So, who was right and who was wrong? The answer is obvious: The resounding response from clients and the industry at large shows that despite the fact that Mike Colón and Jonathan Canlas were running toward different end zones, both teams still won. Their success on the outside was a mirror image of their authentic success on the inside.

Authenticity is always right, because when we act on ideas that we are authentically passionate about, we experience higher levels of fulfillment. This causes us to approach decisions and tasks with greater energy, more creativity, and a higher level of enthusiasm—and the natural by-product of such qualities and behaviors is greater overall success.

Your goals are not going to be other people's goals, and that's okay. You are inherently far more capable than you think. Trust your authentic instinct and pursue projects and ideas that are in accordance with *your* authentic life goals.

Authentic Freedom

At its most primal level, the search for authenticity is the search to improve your life. I promise that in authenticity, you will find the transformation you seek.

Life is short. There's no time to be paralyzed by fear, dammed up by pride, or derailed by procrastination. By being your true, authentic self—the self that is outside the egg—you can be free. You will discover the power to live a meaningful and successful life. A life filled with happiness. A life free from regret.

Imagine what your life would be like if you were completely uninhibited by fear, pride, or procrastination.

What would you be capable of?

Anything.

SERVE

THANK

ASK

RECEIVE

TRUST

12

The 5 Actions of the New Smart: Serve, Thank, Ask, Receive, Trust

He drew a circle that shut me out—
Heretic, rebel, a thing to flout.
But Love and I had the wit to win:
We drew a circle that took him in!
—EDWIN MARKHAM, POET

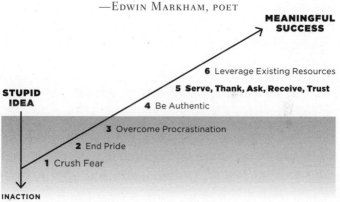

MEANINGFUL SUCCESS

6 Leverage Existing Resources
5 Serve, Thank, Ask, Receive, Trust
STUPID IDEA
4 Be Authentic
3 Overcome Procrastination
2 End Pride
1 Crush Fear

INACTION

His head was reeling. There he stood, all five-foot-five of him, unable to think of a single question to ask. It was the very beginning of his career as a new lawyer, and he couldn't even muster the courage to cross-examine a witness in court. "I stood up," he recalled, "but

my heart sank into my boots." He had failed at his very
first case. He sat back down, told the client he should
hire new representation, and returned his fee.

He then applied to be a high school teacher. He was
not hired for the position. Again, he had failed.

How did this scared, little man, who described himself as "depressed" and "exasperated" because of his
many failures, go on to influence the lives of millions, including the works of Mother Teresa, Martin Luther King
Jr., John F. Kennedy, Albert Einstein, Nelson Mandela,
and countless others? How did he go from failure to being hailed and even reverenced as the father of a *nation*?
Mahatma Gandhi succeeded because he understood the
very real power of starting something stupid.

Years earlier, long before his humiliating failure
in the courtroom, Gandhi's high school teacher once
prompted him to cheat. Noticing that he had misspelled
a word on his spelling test, the teacher discreetly encouraged Gandhi to copy the word from the student next
to him. But Gandhi's conscience wouldn't allow it. In
Gandhi's own words, "The result was that all of the boys
except myself were found to have spelt every word cor-
rectly. Only I had been stupid," Gandhi recalled. "The
teacher tried later to bring this stupidity home to me, but
without effect. I could never learn the art of 'copying.'"

Gandhi was unaffected by the teacher's chastisement

because he knew his decision was right, and he could not be swayed. Gandhi understood how to operate from his authentic core, a core governed by integrity. From a young age, Gandhi knew how to courageously push through the disparaging opinions of others in order to embrace the New Smart, and he would continue to do so for the rest of his life—creating a ripple of positive change that would be felt across the world.

> *"Only I had been stupid."*
> —MAHATMA GANDHI

Gandhi's defining moment occurred years later in a train station in South Africa. He had just boarded a train and taken his ticketed seat in first class when another passenger began to complain about Gandhi's presence in the car. An official was promptly called, and Gandhi was ordered to "go to the van compartment" with the other "coloured" passengers. When he refused, stating that he had purchased a first class ticket, he was thrown from the train, and the authorities seized his luggage.

It was winter. His overcoat was packed away in his confiscated bag. Gandhi spent the night shivering in a cold waiting room with no light. It was here, in these lowly circumstances that Gandhi faced his defining moment: "Should I fight for my rights or go back to India?" Gandhi pondered the decision that lay before him, and as he did, his sense of purpose grew stronger. He was fueled significantly by his degrading experience on the train—an experience Gandhi knew was not an isolated incident, but a regular occurrence for all Indians living in South Africa at the time.

"The hardship to which I was subjected was superficial," he said, "only a symptom of the deep disease of colour prejudice. I should try if possible, to root out the disease and suffer hardships in the process." Gandhi's deep-seated integrity would allow him no other option than to do what was *right*. The odds may have been against him, conventional wisdom might have called him crazy, but he was willing to endure whatever it took to "root out the disease." Gandhi was willing to do whatever it took to fulfill what was soon to become his life's mission—Gandhi was ready to embrace the New Smart.

START: Creating Your Inner Circle of Success

In the wake of failure, and despite the many challenges he would yet be called upon to endure, the story of Gandhi is a perfect demonstration of everything it means to embrace the New Smart. Gandhi's courageous life exemplifies what I call the principles of START, or the 5 Actions of the New Smart.

As mentioned earlier, START is an acronym that stands for **S**erve, **T**hank, **A**sk, **R**eceive, and **T**rust. These principles may seem trite or naïve, even juvenile, but if properly embraced, STARTing changes the game. When you serve, thank, ask, receive, and trust, you position yourself to authentically connect with the people around you. In so doing, you can effectively create a deep, wide, and lasting impact for good, and exponentially accelerate your path toward meaningful, purpose-driven success. In business and in life, engaging others through the principles of START grants you the opportunity to showcase your competence and demonstrate that you are worthy of trust and respect (across your department, organization, industry, market, community, family, or, in Gandhi's case, the world).

The power of START is twofold. First, of course, we have the acronym START which helps us to commit to memory the principles—serve, thank, ask, receive, and trust—and second, we have *start* as a verb.

Start as a verb is *why* the principles are so effective. The power of *start* as a verb lies in the simple act of *starting*. When we go, move, or begin, we unleash the simple yet profound power of momentum. Once your project is in motion, you'll find that one thing moves very rapidly to another. But while the idea of momentum is fairly intoxicating, it doesn't answer the bigger questions of *how to begin* and *where to begin?* Well, in the story of Gandhi, he started small and chose to begin with what was right in front of him.

Gandhi started with service. Almost immediately after his experience on the train, he decided that his primary focus would be to "get in touch" with every Indian in Pretoria. So with the help of an acquaintance, Gandhi organized a meeting. Then, despite his crippling fear of speaking in public, Gandhi courageously stood before the Indians of Pretoria and delivered the first public speech of his life. Gandhi had developed an authentic purpose that was even stronger than his fear. (Gandhi went on to be proclaimed by many as one of the greatest orators in history.)

Gandhi continued to serve his new friends. At the first meeting held in Pretoria, Gandhi had noticed how few in the audience spoke English. Feeling that the language would be useful to them, he began to teach English for free to any who expressed interest. All the while, Gandhi continued to reach out to his people by holding community meetings. Before long, Gandhi recalled, "the result was that there was now in Pretoria no Indian I did not know, or whose condition I was not acquainted with."

Gandhi STARTed. He didn't procrastinate his mission with less important things. He set aside personal pride, humbly sacrificed, and then asked others to do the same. He didn't shrink from his circumstances. He worked with the limited experiences and resources he had available to him, and he frequently leveraged the talents of others to maintain his momentum, openly expressing gratitude all along the way. Because of the reputation Gandhi had established through his consistent service and commitment to people and purpose, his followers trusted him to the point that they "would rather die than break their word" to Gandhi.

As we engage the principles of START and connect authentically with others, we draw closer to our dreams than we ever could on our own. When we overcome fear, pride, and procrastination, when we become authentic and live the principles of service, thanks, asking, receiving, and extending trust, we create an unyielding foundation for future success.

SERVE
OTHERS

*"Successful people are always looking for op-
portunities to help others. Unsuccessful people
are always asking, 'What's in it for me?'"*
—BRIAN TRACY, BESTSELLING AUTHOR AND BUSINESS
COACH

After following his morning routine in his comfortable
home, Craig Kielburger made his way downstairs to the
breakfast table and poured himself a bowl of cereal. He
picked up the newspaper and read the headline "Battled
Child Labour, Boy, 12, Murdered."

He was jolted. "Some people's lives are transformed gradually," Kielburger would later say. "Others
are changed in an instant." That morning, he happened
across a headline from the *Toronto Star,* and Kielburger's
life would never be the same. "ISLAMABAD, Pakistan

(AP): When Iqbal Masih was 4 years old," the article read, "his parents sold him into slavery for less than $16. For the next six years, he remained shackled to a carpet-weaving loom most of the time, tying tiny knots hour after hour. By the age of 12, he was free and traveling the world in his crusade against the horrors of child labor."

Kielburger was horrified to learn that Iqbal had been murdered. "Shot dead," according to the article. "Some believe his murder was carried out by angry members of the carpet industry who had made repeated threats to silence the young activist."

Kielburger was overwhelmed with questions about Iqbal, his parents, and child labor in general. After a visit to the public library, where he made copies of every magazine and newspaper article he could find on the subject, Kielburger decided he had to do something. He started with a simple phone call that led to several subsequent calls to human rights organizations. Not only was Kielburger surprised by how little these organizations knew about child labor, but he was amazed that despite the fact that this was an issue that "was all about children, there were no young people involved in these organizations. . . . Shouldn't other children be speaking out in defense of children?" he thought.

So Kielburger asked a local seventh-grade teacher, Mr. Fedrigoni, if he could have a few minutes to speak to the students before class. He told the students Iqbal's story and then said, "So this is the issue. I don't know a lot about it, but I want to learn more. Maybe some of us could start a group to look at it together. Who wants to join?" Kielburger organized a meeting that was attended by a total of twelve seventh graders, and Free the Children was born.

A year later, Kielburger took a trip to Asia to see the effects of child labor firsthand. While there, he learned that the Canadian prime minister would be in the area for a trade delegation, but he was denied time to speak with him. So, Kielburger held a media conference that was attended by the major Canadian television and news outlets that had been following the prime minister's trip. The media ate it up. The story of Craig Kielburger upstaging the prime minister was carried by major news networks all over the world, including CNN. "Within no time," Kielburger recalled, "the prime minister's handlers were looking for me. . . . The meeting went well and ended with the prime minister agreeing to bring up the issue of child labor with the heads of South Asian governments."

At the time of Craig Kielburger's meeting with the Canadian prime minister, he had just turned thirteen.

"Everybody can be great . . . because anybody can serve."

—MARTIN LUTHER KING JR.

When Kielburger came across the headline that changed his life forever, he had been picking up the newspaper to read the comics, and the first place Kielburger arranged to speak about Iqbal was in front of his very own seventh-grade class. Kielburger, along with that tiny group of his classmates, had been so inspired by the story of Iqbal—another twelve-year-old child who had lived 7,000 miles away—that together, they changed the world.

According to the Free the Children website, to date the organization has built more than 650 schools that educate more than 55,000 children every day. Additionally:

- Over 207,000 health kits have been sent to children in need.
- Their leadership training programs motivate more than 350,000 young people a year to serve others.
- One million people now have improved access to water, health care, and sanitation.
- More than 30,000 women are self-sufficient from their microloan program.

Even Oprah's Angel Network teamed up with Free the Children to build almost sixty schools in underdeveloped countries. Oprah invited Craig and his brother Marc to launch the "O Ambassadors Project" on her show.

And it all STARTed with a twelve-year-old boy eating a bowl of cereal.

The Power of Service

Not only are there inherent blessings available to us when we serve others—the "helper's high" as one example—but serving is a powerful way to strategically connect with people and an effective way to start anything you want to do. Like a boomerang, the service you throw out will come right back at you—often in surprising ways.

> *"You can't help someone get up a hill without getting closer to the top yourself."*
> —GENERAL NORMAN SCHWARZKOPF,
>   RETIRED US ARMY GENERAL

The key ingredient in engaging the power available from service is motive. Service that is performed with the aim *only* to receive in return will be unsuccessful every time. Serving strictly for personal gain is a thinly veiled attempt to selfishly take from someone else. It is inauthentic, outside of integrity, and has the potential to destroy relationships before they're even begun.

That's not to say we can't strategically select the types of projects we want to pursue and hope for a favorable outcome that is aligned with our personal goals. However, there can be no *absolute expectation* of such. As we learn from Gandhi, "The moment there is suspicion about a person's motives, everything he does becomes tainted."

> *"It is literally true that you can succeed best and quickest by helping others to succeed."*
> —NAPOLEON HILL, AUTHOR OF *THINK AND GROW RICH*

If approached authentically, service is a *highly* successful way to propel us toward our goals—the power available from the residual effects of service is absolutely unlimited.

Service is one of the most effective ways to overcome the Time-Education-Money Gap (TEM Gap) and get started on your goals—no matter the circumstances. Service has very little barrier to entry. Offering selfless service is an effective way to get your foot in the door in areas where you might not be able to otherwise.

As we serve others, we effectively embrace the Humble Power Alternative. Not only does service help us develop our humility, it gives us an opportunity to strategically showcase both our most powerful strengths and our capacity for effective leadership. Referring back to Collins' example from *Good to Great,* serving others is powerful evidence to the ones we serve of our resolve "to do whatever it takes to make the company [or the project or the person] great, no matter how big or hard the decisions."

Service is a powerful way to establish rapport, demonstrate credibility, and earn trust. When we serve, we get to know the people we are working with (serving) in unique ways. When we develop meaningful connections with the ones we serve, they are eager and willing to help us achieve our highest potential for success.

Through serving, we learn. When we are serving in our area of interest, or under people we really respect, we are given a unique opportunity to learn for free and gain experience without risk.

1. *Free experience.* You don't have to pay to serve someone else, and if you work things out effectively, you could be given the opportunity to learn invaluable lessons and skills in your area of interest at no cost to you.

2. *Risk-free learning.* Experience sometimes comes at a cost, but when you're gaining experience in a service capacity, the stakes aren't quite as high. This isn't to say you should do sloppy work (that would defeat the purpose). When serving others you should put your heart and soul into the project. Go above and beyond. Serve like everything depended on you to succeed. It's been my experience

that when you excel in "free" service, unexpected opportunities open for you to excel in the paid arena too.

Service allows you to start projects that could potentially progress into something more. When we approach people we want to serve with a project we think will bless their businesses and/or lives, not only does it show initiative, but it gives you the opportunity to test your idea in the market. If your project works, you never know, you just might make a dream come true.

Go. Give. Get.

Steve Hargadon, founder of FutureOfEducation.com once told me that his motto is "Go. Give. Get." He explains,

> Go: Start doing something you love and value enough that you'd do it for free in your spare time. Give: Find a way to really help people, to do something that will make a difference in their lives. Get: Notice that the opportunity for benefits will come your way—either financially, or just in the satisfaction of helping make the world a better place.

These are the principles of service he used to start Classroom 2.0, a social networking site for educators that critics said would be a flop. The site now has over 70,000 members from 195 countries, and Hargadon runs virtual conferences attended by over 100,000 people annually.

He says that starting with service "reshaped my career, and has led to an amazing number of opportunities to do good things for people I care about and opportunities to get paid to do what I love."

Whatever your idea, start with service. Do it without a hidden agenda, and always be transparent about serving for serving's sake or serving to help make your idea happen.

Serve, and watch where it takes you.

"Gratitude is not only the greatest of the virtues, but the parent of all of the others."
—CICERO

When I think of the importance of gratitude in general, but specifically as a catalyst for success, I can't help but nod eagerly in agreement. Gratitude is a remarkable force for good in all aspects of life, and I'm not the only one who thinks so:

"A noble person is mindful and thankful of the favors he receives from others."—Buddha

"Cultivate the habit of being grateful for every good thing that comes to you, and to give thanks continuously. And because all things have contributed to your advancement, you should include all things in your gratitude."—Wallace D. Wattles

"Of all the 'attitudes' we can acquire, surely the attitude of gratitude is the most important, and by far the most life-changing."—Zig Ziglar

"When you are grateful, fear disappears and abundance appears."—Anthony Robbins

The following two stories serve to demonstrate the deep importance of gratitude in increasing success.

The Pizza Parable

The first story took place on the streets of a major city, late one snowy winter night. I was attending a professional leadership training with some friends and colleagues. Hungry from a long day of training, we asked the concierge at the hotel for a recommendation for dinner. He referred us to a pizza joint that served *massive*-sized gourmet pizzas (the kind that college students go crazy over).

For a small fortune, we ordered the largest pizza on the menu, and had it delivered to our hotel. The pizza was so big that five ravenous adult men couldn't put away even a third of it. We didn't want the leftover food to go to waste, so we decided to give it away. We wandered around town until we came to a nearby train station where a group of homeless people had gathered for shelter from the wintry cold. What happened next was interesting.

Though we were some distance away, the group of people chatting in the station quieted down and fixed their eyes on me as I approached and asked if they would like the pizza.

Without saying a word, one of the men swiftly yanked the box from my hands and turned back to his friends. They huddled together, eating the pizza as fast as they could. It was as if I had never been there at all.

A Tale of Two Twenties

Sometime later, my wife found herself on the same snowy city streets shopping with some friends. A homeless woman with a teenage boy in tow approached them. The boy stood off to the side, clearly humiliated by the exchange he knew was about to take place.

"Do you have any spare change?" the woman quietly asked.

Sensing the complete desperation in her voice, my wife and her friends offered a twenty-dollar bill to the woman. She immediately expressed genuine surprise and deep gratitude at the offering, so much so that the group pooled another twenty dollars and handed it to the woman.

She thanked them again and again, and as she turned to leave, the woman had tears in her eyes, and the teenage boy, whom they could only assume was her son, had a smile of complete gratitude stretching from ear to ear.

The Power of Gratitude

Note the profound lessons illustrated by the two stories.

Lack of gratitude limits future gifts. When the homeless men in the train station received the pizza, they didn't express gratitude. They didn't even say a word, let alone acknowledge the gift in any way. Author G. B. Stern once noted, "Silent gratitude isn't much use to anyone."

Clearly, not saying "thank you" because you're hungry is a prime example of Abraham Maslow's famed Hierarchy of Needs. Maslow's theory is that humans are motivated by unsatisfied needs, which he called "deficiency needs." In other words, certain basic physiological needs like breathing, nutrition, clothes, and shelter must be met before a person can move toward filling other needs like safety, love and belonging, esteem, and self-actualization. The fact that the homeless men didn't say thank you for the food didn't necessarily denote the absence of gratitude; it could have simply meant an overpowering presence of intense hunger.

But, while being hungry may be an excuse for others, it is no excuse for *you* or *me*. How eager and willing are you to lend an ungrateful person a hand? How authentically invested do you feel in their goals and overall success? Ungrateful people are no fun. Don't let that ungrateful person *ever* be you.

If you want to increase success, don't discount other people's contributions by not sufficiently acknowledging them.

> **Don't be so hungry for success that you forget to thank the people around you.**

Gratitude brings greater gifts. When the homeless woman in the story expressed sincere gratitude, my wife and her friends felt immediate and sincere gratification from the good they had done in her life. This inspired them to want to do even more to help.

Adam Smith, in his work entitled *Theory of Moral Sentiments,* wrote, "The sentiment which most immediately and directly prompts us to reward, is gratitude." It's true.

Thanking is a form of payment that exponentially pays forward both personally and professionally. People are far more likely to collaborate with, hire, or refer a grateful person than an ungrateful one. Additionally, experts on positive psychology have shown that the trait of gratitude actually increases overall happiness and decreases depression.

> *"Gratitude has the potential to change everything from its ordinary state to being a gift."*
> —BARBARA FREDERICKSON, PSYCHOLOGIST

In order to build genuine relationships, experience greater fulfillment, and set yourself up for significant and meaningful success, always express sincere gratitude, no matter how small or seemingly insignificant the contribution may be.

Gratitude Grows

If you want to experience a greater sense of thankfulness in your life, say "Thank you!" more often. It's a small thing, but people who consistently express gratitude develop a higher level of awareness for all the things in their lives they have to be grateful for. When we express our gratitude, it grows.

"Asking is the beginning of receiving. Make sure you don't go to the ocean with a tea-spoon. At least take a bucket so the kids won't laugh at you."

—JIM ROHN, RENOWNED AUTHOR AND SPEAKER

When I first met Justin Lyon, it was immediately apparent that he was unlike anyone I'd ever known. "Charismatic" is a heavily diluted description. So when Lyon told me he hadn't always been that way, it was a shocking revelation to say the least. When he described what he was like growing up, he used words like "shy" and "insecure."

Lyon had always wanted to work in the movie industry. He pictured himself producing independent films and changing the world. However, in the small town in Idaho where he grew up . . . well, to say his dream was frowned upon would be an understatement. "It's devil's work!" was essentially the response. So he put his dream away. "My culture told me that going into filmmaking would be foolish," he recalls, "so I stopped dreaming about it."

A few years later, Lyon moved to Arizona where he was hired as a bellboy at a luxury resort. He quickly worked his way up the hierarchy and was promoted to the position of Bell Captain. The other full-time Bell Captains were in their forties and fifties, and frequently discussed where they'd be now if they had made different decisions when they were younger. The regret these men openly expressed made a deep impression on young Lyon, who was in his early twenties at the time. "Do I want to make this job into a career?" he thought.

Lyon did his job well; he always served cheerfully and took a genuine interest in each hotel guest. In turn, guests often took a genuine interest in him—and celebrity guests were no exception. It wasn't uncommon for him to wait on people who made headlines. Actors,

musicians, and even movie producers frequented the resort. With the other bellmen's regrets ringing loudly in
his ears, Lyon remembered his dream of working in the
movie industry and decided he was ready to do whatever
it took.

He worked up the courage to discuss his dream
with celebrity guests by reasoning with himself: *We're
all human, and famous people are just humans who are
better known.* He opened up to these guests, and many
of them took a genuine interest in him. Over time, his
paradigm began to change. One day, he asked a visit-
ing studio executive from Los Angeles about his concern
that the industry would make him corrupt. The executive responded, "You can be corrupt at anything. There
are corrupt lawyers, dentists, and doctors too. You can
make it in this industry and still be yourself."

Lyon later related, "I learned that if you love something, if your heart is really in it, you can live your
dreams and maintain your ideals."

He was done waiting. In his own Hollywood-worthy
moment, he quit his job, packed his bags, and headed for
LA. After he arrived, he placed a call to Mark Mulcahy,
a VP at Paramount Pictures whom Lyon had met while
he was bellhopping. Lyon asked Mulcahy if he would
take him on a tour of the Paramount studio. He said yes,

and Lyon got to see behind the scenes and get a better idea of what it really took to make movies.

Next, Lyon cold-called one of his idols, producer Gerry Molen, who had produced *Schindler's List* alongside director Steven Spielberg. Lyon told Molen that he was an aspiring producer and asked him for advice. Molen graciously agreed to part with some nuggets of wisdom for the industry. He advised Lyon to go to school, but not to let that stop him from producing along the way. So, Lyon enrolled at the Art Center College of Design and started doing as many projects as he could. He remembers, "These projects had shoestring, rather, no-string budgets," so he volunteered his time.

One day, Lyon was contacted by Christian Jacobs, "The MC Bat Commander" from the popular rock band The Aquabats, and Scott Schultz, an accomplished artist and musician. "They were sick of boring TV programming for kids," he recalls. "They wanted to create an educational children's show that was fun for parents, too." The problem was, the pair had been pitching their idea to networks for six years with no results. "They had their own unique talents and backgrounds," Lyon said, "but they were not finding success getting their children's show picked up by a network."

Because Lyon had taken Gerry Molen's advice and started working right away, he already had enough

projects under his belt to legitimize himself as a producer. So the three of them started a production company called The Magic Store, and got to work. Again
remembering Molen's advice, Lyon decided to just bite
the bullet and make some pilot episodes. Luckily, Lyon
had learned how to bootstrap from his early projects,
and the team was able to convince family and friends to
make costumes, create the music, and design the sets for
the show. They figured, worst-case scenario, they could
recoup the little money they borrowed by selling some
DVDs.

Once the pilots were complete, they resumed the
process of pitching the show to the networks. Nothing.
Then the game changed. They decided to upload a trailer
to the Internet to see if there was any interest. The video
went viral. Over a four-day period, there were over a million views, crashing their server.

"Suddenly," Lyon said, "people from television networks started e-mailing us every five minutes, from all
around the world, asking us where they could find our
show." At the same time they were fielding all these
calls, viewers started calling Nickelodeon, suggesting
they pick up the show. Even Jared Hess, the director of
Napoleon Dynamite and *Nacho Libre,* called the director
of Nickelodeon Movies and told her she needed to see
the pilot.

Yo Gabba Gabba went into production just a couple of months later, and within four seasons, it has become a household name. Brands like Vans have licensed *Yo Gabba Gabba* shoes; Volcom licensed T-shirts; Neff licensed beanies, and on and on. The show has even done live performances, selling out Radio City Music Hall in New York City.

All because of two dads with a stupid idea they weren't willing to give up on, and a shy kid from a small town in Idaho, who wasn't afraid to ask for help in achieving his big-city dreams.

> *"A man may fulfill the object of his existence by asking a question he cannot answer, and attempting a task he cannot achieve."*
> —OLIVER WENDELL HOLMES

A simple but effective way to become who you want to become or go where you want to go is to ask for directions from those who have already been there.

We've all been in the car with a driver who won't stop and ask for directions. In fact, we've probably all *been* that driver. "I'm almost there. I can figure it out. Just one more exit." These are the same types of things people tell themselves when they're stuck on a project and are headed nowhere fast.

What stops us from asking for what we need? Here's an example to illustrate.

There is a movie theater near my home that always has the *longest* lines. Moviegoers are consistently in line for as long as half an hour and many frequently miss the beginning of their movies. Yet right inside the door of the building (before you hand over your ticket), there is a ticket kiosk. You simply insert a debit or credit card, and the machine prints your movie pass right there. No one is ever at this machine. Anyone can walk in, pay, and go straight to their show without waiting more than thirty seconds. All the line-waiters have to do is ask if there is a faster way to get a ticket. But no one does.

Many times we don't ask simply because we are *assuming* that there's no other way. We shrug our shoulders and sigh, "This is just the way it is." But more often than not, we're wrong!

Don't underestimate the power of asking. Get out of line and start asking questions. It will accelerate your success.

How to Ask: Mission Matching

Asking is scary. No one wants to be rejected or come off sounding presumptuous or needy, but asking is the quickest way to get from where you are to where you want to be! And there are respectful and compelling ways to ask for help, ways that will honor and even excite the person you are asking, and maybe even inspire them to *want* to help you along your way.

I call this kind of asking *Mission Matching*.

Mission Matching requires you to ask for things that create synergistic congruence between missions. In other words, Mission Matching means that whatever you're asking, the proposition needs to be executed in a way that is mutually, rather than exclusively, beneficial. You're not just going to ask and receive; your aim is to ask, receive, and contribute as well.

Before you approach the person you will be asking for help, consider these three points:

Do your homework. Research the person or organization you're approaching in order to determine their specific needs, goals, and potential struggles.

Ask "What's in it for them?" Explore how you can use your unique strengths to contribute to their overarching mission in the most significant ways.

Match your missions. Determine how working together can serve both of you in ways that are mutually and significantly beneficial.

Asking for help in this way is not only beneficial to your long-term success, it's often even *more* powerful than simply hiring people or companies for their services. There is often no exchange of money, but there is generally a more significant *emotional* exchange. This creates the potential for a deep and lasting relationship and opens up opportunities for future collaboration.

One of the Fastest Growing YouTube Channels in the World

My friend Devin Graham is a powerful example of the way Mission Matching accelerates success.

Graham's out-of-this-world-amazing weekly installations to his YouTube channel have already acquired tens of millions of views, and those numbers are steadily climbing every day. At the time of this writing, he has one of the fastest growing YouTube channels in the world. Not only does his diehard fan base eagerly anticipate and then frantically share each new video he posts, but he is continually being contacted to work on well-paying gigs for major brands, celebrities, and even the government. He is living his dream, and so much more.

So, how did he do it? In his own words,

> It all comes down to one thing. I work with brands and collaborate with people with similar interests. That allows for other people to fund my ideas, which makes it possible with a zero dollar budget. What most people don't know is that every brand that I have worked for to this point in my career, as

far as videos that appear on my YouTube channel go,
I have done for free.

Why would such a fiercely talented artist give away
his time for free? Well, Graham understands the remarkable power and value of Mission Matching. "The way I
saw it," Devin relates, "if I could get someone else to pay
for the production of my videos, the quality would be
much greater than just me trying to do it on my own,"
and a quality portfolio leads to higher paying opportunities in Graham's future.

Meanwhile, the individuals, brands, and musicians
he collaborates with benefit by getting amazing promo-
tional material at cost—not to mention the free marketing they receive when Graham posts their movies to his
YouTube channel. "Without these collaborations," he says,
"there is no way I would have been able to get to where
I am." Graham started small, with simple projects and
no-name brands, to build his reputation. "I made a couple
of these sorts of videos . . . to build my own credibility,"
he relates. Then he approached bigger brands he thought
would be interested in the kinds of videos he was already
producing, and offered to make videos for them for free.

After eighteen months of solid, exhaustive work, he
says he's finally in a position "where I can charge companies and brands what I want for them to get featured in

one of my videos. Yes, we are still collaborating, but now I can make a living from it. . . . Now that I have established a voice, I can . . . make the videos I want . . . with the companies and people I want."

Through the process of Mission Matching—using his unique talents to serve others in mutually beneficial ways—Graham has moved mountains, made waves, and influenced the world in major ways. People told him he was stupid and crazy and that it would be impossible for him to make it in the film industry. But through ingenuity and his own blood, sweat, and tears, Devin Graham continually does what others say is impossible. And he is living a life without regret.

Expect a Yes; Respect the No

You won't always get the answer you're hoping for. But that's okay. Be gracious and consider this saying: "Remember that not getting what you want is sometimes a wonderful stroke of luck." Each *no* means you're one *no* closer to your *yes*.

RECEIVE
OTHERS

*"A hundred times every day I remind myself
that my inner and outer life are based on the
labors of other men, living and dead, and that
I must exert myself in order to give in the
same measure as I have received and am still
receiving."*
—ALBERT EINSTEIN

One day, after a long morning at the beach, I went to
start my car only to realize I had run out of gas. I headed
down the street toward the nearest gas station and asked
the attendant if he had a gas can I could borrow. Before
he could answer, the stranger in line behind me spoke
up and said that he had a full gas can in his van that I
could use.

At that moment I'd been offered a gift. I needed help, and a stranger had come to my rescue. But I wanted to say no. In a split second, a million reasons I didn't want this stranger's help passed through my mind. I told myself I could do it on my own, that I didn't want to inconvenience him, that it would be awkward to receive help from a stranger. However, I reminded myself of the power of receiving, and told myself to give it a go.

I thanked the stranger over and over while apologizing profusely for the inconvenience. To add to my already heightened feelings of awkwardness, it turned out that he was originally headed in the opposite direction. The stranger, however, was unaffected by this revelation and still cheerfully insisted on driving me back to my car.

When I climbed into his van and looked around, two things were immediately evident: one, the man was a struggling landscaper, and two, he loved to fish. Rusty landscaping equipment, dozens of old fishing poles, and the strong aroma of dead fish filled the back of the van. He told me that he and his coworker had just finished fishing and were now headed to a job. When I asked about his work, he explained how he'd recently lost a lot of income but was optimistic. "I'll never be rich," he said, with bright, happy eyes, "but it gets me by."

He took me to my car, and I humbly put this stranger's gas into my tank. But my car was parked at a very steep angle, so even the amount of gas from the full gas can wasn't enough. The car still wouldn't start. I felt horrible. I was so embarrassed to be further inconveniencing this nice stranger.

Again, he was unaffected; in fact, the stranger was genuinely happy to help. On our way back to the gas station, I noticed that *his* empty light was on. I was surprised he hadn't run out of gas trying to help me! It suddenly occurred to me: this stranger wasn't at the gas station to fill up his van—he didn't have enough money to do that—he was there to fill up the gas can for his landscaping equipment . . . the very gas can he had so generously offered to me.

As I finished filling the small gas can, I then turned to the stranger and I offered *him* a gift.

"I want to put some gas in your van," I said.

He shook his head no. "Karma," he smiled. "It always comes back to help me. That's how I've gotten by all these years." He continued adamantly, "I didn't help you to profit."

I understood his feelings, but believing that karmic law was surely reciprocating his kindness right here and now, I insisted and filled up his van. This stranger's gift to me had been returned to him tenfold—unexpectedly and immediately.

The Gift, the Giver, and the Gifted

Who was the giver? Who was the receiver? What was the gift? The gift from the landscaper was much more than just gas—it was selfless concern for me. This man had selflessly done for me what I could not have done for myself, and in turn, I was eager to do for him what he could not have done for himself. Our roles had reversed, and we both became receivers that day. I drove away from that experience feeling happy, thankful and inspired, and I know my new friend did too.

When we graciously receive from others, everyone wins. Maybe not in such immediate or obvious ways, but our willingness to receive from another blesses both the giver and the receiver.

Get Open

In football, one of the most important positions is the receiver. In the 1975–76 division playoff game, the Dallas Cowboys were down 14 to 10 against the Minnesota Vikings. With only twenty-four seconds left on the clock in the fourth quarter, the Cowboys' quarterback Roger Staubach threw a desperation long-bomb pass from midfield to wide receiver Drew Pearson, who caught it on the five-yard line and ran into the end zone to seal their victory.

Staubach said that when he threw the ball to Pearson, "I closed my eyes and said a Hail Mary." When the ball came to Pearson, he got open and barely caught the ball by trapping it against his right hip. It was a difficult catch, but Pearson hung on, ran with it, and scored. It was this play that coined the term "a Hail Mary pass," and it has since become one of the most famous plays in NFL history.

On occasion, I am fascinated by my own propensity toward turning down gifts. When things (or opportunities) that I need, want, and/or have been secretly (or openly) hoping for arrive in my life, I often have to fight the urge to immediately turn them away. After much introspection, I've realized something about myself: no matter how badly I want or need the gift, I am often unhappy or uncomfortable with the way it is delivered. I tend to become overrun with pride, embarrassment, or discomfort that keeps me from accepting what I have been offered—even if the gift is the very thing or assistance I most want and need in my life.

Just like the football analogy, it's not always easy to get open enough to receive the things, the help, or the advice that we need. There are a million things that get in our way, and pride is at the root of many of them. If we are serious about success, however, we must overcome our qualms with the method of delivery, we must overcome the discomfort we feel, sometimes by swallowing our pride, and we must graciously receive the opportunities that are offered to us.

> *"And, when you want something, all the universe conspires in helping you to achieve it."*
> —PAULO COELHO, AUTHOR OF *THE ALCHEMIST*

In order to receive, we must get open.

Accepting vs. Receiving

I have given my children countless toys that they've never really used—or toys they have used once or twice and then discarded deep in the abyss of their toy closet, never to been seen or heard from again. Then I'll hear, "Daad, I'm boored. There's nothing to plaaaaay with." I just shake my head as I think of the closets in each of their rooms, filled with the ability to turn any regular old Saturday afternoon into Christmas morning. Did my kids really *receive* those gifts? Or did they just *get* them, did they just *accept* them?

Often times, even daily, we are offered gifts in the form of opportunity. Do we recognize them as such? And do we really receive them when they show up in our lives? When you are offered a gift, you essentially have three choices: reject, accept, or receive.

Reject. When you are offered a gift and you reject

it, you are slamming the door on your potential for future success. You are essentially saying that you want your pride more than you want your dreams.

Accept. When you are offered a gift and you accept it, but then simply set it on the shelf, that is not *receiving*. That is getting, and it is selfish and one-sided (and often prideful as well).

Receive. To truly receive, you must take the gift and run with it—achieve your goals, make your project succeed, seal the victory!

Can you imagine how history would have changed for the Cowboys if Pearson hadn't been able to get open? Or if he had gotten open, but then dropped the ball? The Cowboys certainly wouldn't have gone on to play in the Super Bowl that year, nor would they have become the first NFC wild-card team in history to do so. Pearson *received* that pass, held it tight, ran, and scored! *That's the power of receiving.*

So when the ball comes your way, don't run away from it.

> **Accepting a gift is a transaction.**
> *Receiving* **a gift means you run with it and score.**

Receiving Is a Gift

Receiving—*genuinely receiving*—is one of the most wonderful gifts you can give to the giver.

If you're like me and your pride sometimes gets in the way of allowing yourself to receive, if you feel selfish, awkward, or downright uncomfortable, remember, you and the giver are on the same team. In the same way Staubach was cheering for Pearson and eagerly anticipating his success, the giver is the one passing you the ball. He *wants* you to receive it, run with it, and score!

When you receive a gift, really receive it; it is a sign of gratitude and respect to the giver. In essence, when you receive the gift, you also receive the giver. They receive the blessing of watching you run and score, and they have the wonderful satisfaction of knowing that they contributed in some small (or large) way to your success. The "R" in START could have been "Receive *from* others." But it's not. It's "Receive others." When people offer you a gift, you're not just receiving a product, a service, or a leg up—you're receiving the giver, and they in turn are receiving you.

Make this your motto: *Receive and be received.* Significant, lasting connections are made when the giver and the receiver graciously, respectfully and simultaneously receive each other. Receiving is often much harder than giving, but when you allow others to serve you, you'll both become edified together.

The Good Receiver

What do people do when they can't get good reception on the radio? They adjust the antenna or station until the sound comes in strong and clear. If they can't find good reception, they'll simply change the station. If your humility, authenticity, and sincere connection to your dreams isn't coming in strong and clear by being a good receiver, the gifts that are available to you are going to move on to the next station. Don't let that happen to you.

- **Receive gratefully.** Return a warm reception and offer sincere appreciation to the giver.
- **Receive graciously.** Show dignity, esteem, and respect for the giver, no matter the gift.
- **Receive gracefully.** Be humble by recognizing and remembering that it was by another's hand (not your own) that you received.

Tune in. The next time a gift is offered to you, be a good receiver.

TRUST
Others!

"Trust is the new black."
—CRAIG NEWMARK, FOUNDER OF CRAIGSLIST

When Michael Abrashoff took command of the destroyer USS *Benfold* in 1997, he was figuratively jumping into some very stormy seas. The sailors "were so unhappy with their lives on board, they literally cheered when [his] predecessor left the ship for the last time."

Abrashoff was determined not to let that happen to him.

Among his primary goals aboard the ship was retention, and it was evident that the "Do exactly what I say, when I say it, no questions, no comments" method employed by his predecessor was not a viable means to that end.

Abrashoff described the crew as nothing more than demoralized at the time he assumed the position of captain of the *Benfold*. Nevertheless, he set his sights on "sailors so engaged in their work, they would perform better than ever," but he didn't initially know how to get there. What could or should he do differently than the previous captain? After all, this was the United States Navy, with all the strict rules and regulations that came along with it.

But Abrashoff was passionately connected to his goals, so he courageously made a decision to lean into the New Smart. He says, "I ran the risk of never getting promoted again. But I realized that the only way to achieve my goals—combat readiness, retention, and trust . . . was rejecting the 225-year-old U.S. Navy way of running things."

He got right to work. He set out on an enormous undertaking, interviewing each and every sailor aboard the ship individually. He relates, "I had come to realize over the course of my career that no commanding officer has a monopoly on a ship's skills and brainpower. There's an astonishing amount of creativity and know-how below decks, just waiting to be unleashed."

During these interviews with his crew, Abrashoff asked for feedback, listened intently, and implemented many ideas that came from his crew. Over time, as he

diligently fostered, encouraged, and made space for individual creative innovation, the morale on the ship changed.
Equally important, Abrashoff balanced the new leadership
style with "very clear boundaries [his] crew couldn't cross"
to maintain discipline—the balance of freedom and discipline helped create trust. The crew soon felt a sense of
ownership over the *Benfold,* a feeling Abrashoff encouraged. "This is your ship," he told the crew. "Many of them
had never been asked to handle the trust and responsibility that [he] was starting to place in them."

There is no better way to relate the ultimate success
of Captain Abrashoff's unconventional methods than
through this story told in the captain's own words.

The *Benfold* is named after Petty Officer Edward
Benfold, who was a corpsman in the Korean War.
In 1952, during a firefight, Benfold was tending to
two wounded Marines when several enemy soldiers
threw grenades into his foxhole. He picked up the
grenades and stormed the oncoming soldiers, blowing
up them and himself. He was posthumously awarded
the congressional Medal of Honor. The two Marines
he saved are still alive. One of them attended the cer-
emony when I assumed command of the *Benfold.*

I never said this to my crew, but I wanted to
make Petty Officer Benfold proud of his ship. I'd like
to think we did. Together we learned how to look out

for one another, just as Benfold looked out for his comrades. Like Benfold, we took enormous risks, and we took them willingly. We never had to make the kind of sacrifice he did, but I firmly believe that any one of us would have if the situation demanded.

How did Abrashoff spur such a monumental change? The answer is, he extended trust. In the captain's own words, "I trusted my crew with my ship and my career." And clearly, that made all the difference.

Trust Is Stupid

Like Captain Abrashoff, we are figuratively in some very stormy seas. We live in a massively fabricated, low-trust world.

"Trust is naïve."

"Trust carries too much risk."

"Trust is stupid."

Is trust risky? You bet, but so is *distrust*. As Stephen M. R. Covey says, "Don't let the 5% or 10% you can't trust tell you about the 90% or 95% that you can."

Trust is more important than ever, in both business and in life. This is one reason why authenticity is so foundationally valuable as it relates to meaningful success. People—consumers, entrepreneurs, executives, employees, coworkers, family members, friends—are desperate to connect with someone they can trust. More than potentially any other governing principle, being trustworthy, and willing to extend trust to others, will set you apart in today's "stormy" global economy.

> *"A high level of trust is the most important feature any open society can possess."*
>
> —THOMAS L. FRIEDMAN, AUTHOR OF *THE WORLD IS FLAT*

"Build from Trust, Not Just Toward It"

Extending trust doesn't imply that you have to divulge your secret competitive advantage to every passerby. Trust is simply about choosing to associate with people who are trustworthy and being a trustworthy person yourself. In short: Trust. And be trusted. Harold MacMillan, former Prime Minister of the United Kingdom, once said, "A man who trusts nobody is apt to be the kind of man nobody trusts."

Edelman is the world's largest independent public relations firm. Each year, it conducts a study called the "Edelman Trust Barometer," examining trust in government, business, media, and NGOs around the world. Richard Edelman, president and CEO of Edelman, says,

> Build from trust, not just toward it. Trust has become more than an outcome, and more than a state of being. It is a vital tool for persuasion, for building

alliances and for implementing change. Trust is the filter through which information is heard and understood. Under the older trust framework, good news was a tool for building trust. Today, trust is a prerequisite for good news to be believed. The Barometer reports that negative information about a distrusted company is believed after 1–2 repetitions, while positive information must be repeated 4–5 times before it's accepted.

With all the noise from so many conflicting voices of opinion, it's harder than ever before to know who to trust. The greatest thing you can do as you prepare to start your stupid project is commit to "build from trust, not toward it." At the most foundational level of any project, you must build from the cornerstone of trust. In both the public and private sector, associate only with people you can trust, and then strive to be the kind of person who is worthy of their trust in return.

> *"In times of constant change, trust becomes the new currency of business."*
> —ANTHONY ROBBINS

4 Ways To Build Trust

1. **Trust yourself first.** I love this quote from Johann Wolfgang von Goethe, "As soon as you

trust yourself, you will know how to live." Don't wait for others to trust you before you trust yourself. If you don't trust yourself, why should others trust you? As Ralph Waldo Emerson said, "Self-trust is the first secret to success." Take a personal inventory: Do you keep commitments to yourself and others? Do you keep confidences when they have been entrusted to you? Do you put in an honest day's work for an honest day's pay? **When you trust yourself, others, in turn, will trust you.**

2. **Be confident.** Trust and confidence go hand in hand. Be confident in yourself, your worth, your ability, and your stupid ideas, and others will place their trust and confidence in you. Push through fear, pride, and procrastination and simply believe in yourself. **Confidence creates trust, and trust creates confidence.**

3. **Be the first to trust others.** Trusting others first makes them feel inspired and motivated. They feel a genuine urge to reciprocate that trust to you and they want to live up to your wonderful expectation of them. On the other hand, when someone distrusts you, do you feel inspired and motivated? Do you feel confident extending trust to them? Of course not. When trust is not

present, emotional and intellectual guards come up. You start to wonder what the other person might be concealing, you question intent, and more. Distrust is a downward spiral of worry, suspicion, and doubt. Instead, take a leap of faith and extend trust first. Ernest Hemingway said, "The best way to find out if you can trust somebody is to trust them."

4. **Be your word.** Almost nothing will destroy trust as fast as dishonesty and broken promises. On the other hand, nothing will build trust as fast as these four simple words: **Do what you say.**

In all you do (in the public and the private sector), work to give people every reason to trust you. In motive, word, and behavior, always be worthy of trust and you will find that trustworthy people—the kind you *really* want on your team—will not only appreciate you, they'll be eager to collaborate on projects and help you reach your goals.

Serving, thanking, asking, and receiving are the fast track to trust in personal and business relationships. Why? Because when we live these principles, we are actively working to build our character, which is the most direct channel to increased feelings of self-worth and confidence and thus competence, productivity, and meaningful success—all of which are at the foundational level of trust.

START: Connecting the Dots

The symphony of serving, thanking, asking, receiving, and trusting is a *powerful* one. Employing the principles of START helps you strategically connect, prove yourself, and get into the game where all the action is. The principles of START are most effective when they are embraced as continuous principles of human connection. They are "continuous principles" because they aren't meant to be approached chronologically. They are meant to be embraced as a way of life, our "first sources" of behavior in both business and life.

We live in a low-touch world. Interaction through electronics is more prevalent than face-to-face human interaction. While connecting with people around the world has never been easier, paradoxically, creating genuine connections and facilitating meaningful relationships has become much, much harder. And it's taking a toll on our success. Dr. Edward M. Hallowell said, "The more isolated we are, the more stressed we become. . . . Fostering connections and reducing fear promote brainpower. When you make time at least every four to six hours for a 'human moment,' a face-to-face exchange with a person you like, you are giving your brain what it needs."

START is about fostering "human moments" and giving our "brain what it needs." When we are fueled by the guiding principles of START, we are prepared to develop meaningful relationships, seize opportunity when it arrives, accelerate success, create trust, give and receive respect, learn valuable things, and contribute to others (and the world) in meaningful ways.

And the most beautiful part is that START is reciprocal! The more you START, the more people will be excited to serve, thank, ask, receive, and trust you. You'll give and receive in abundance: all because you had the courage to START! These timeless principles are the mechanics of a sustainable foundation for success, no matter the project, and *anyone* can start this way. *Anyone.*

I'd like to add one final level of insight to START by expanding Gavin's Law: Live to start. Start to live.

Live to START	START to live
Live to serve.	Serve to live.
Live to thank.	Thank to live.
Live to ask.	Ask to live.
Live to receive.	Receive to live.
Live to trust.	Trust to live.

Yes, when you live to START, you really will START to live.

> *"You don't have to be great to start, but you have to start to be great."*
>
> —JOE SABAH, AUTHOR AND SPEAKER

MOVE THE WORLD

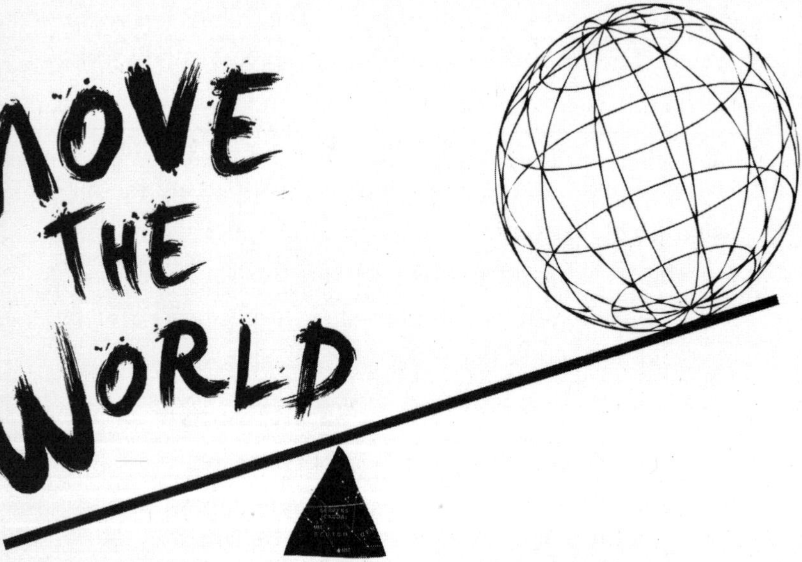

13

Leverage Existing Resources: How to Make Moccasins for a Kardashian and Do Anything Else You Want to Do

"Give me a place to stand, and I shall move the Earth."
—Archimedes

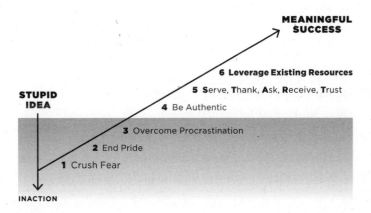

C hris and Susan Petersen were struggling to make ends meet. They had just welcomed their first child, a daughter, into their lives, and the bills inherent to starting a new family had begun to mount.

Chris was a student at the time, however, and,

desperate to get his growing family on their feet, he took a job between semesters installing windows. Susan dreamed of the stability and freedom that financial security could provide. She filled the time while Chris was at work, caring for the couple's then nine-month-old daughter and racking her brain for ways she could supplement their income from home.

"I wasn't falling for the 'stay-at-home-get-rich-quick' ads I saw on the Internet," Susan recalls, "but I knew there had to be a way for me to care for my daughter and make money in my spare time." One day, she overheard someone talking about "making stuff and selling it online." That sounded interesting enough. Susan decided to give it a shot. She didn't consider herself a particularly artistic person, she recalls, "but I did have a sewing machine and could follow a pattern."

Susan decided to make leather goods, such as purses and wallets. The only problem was, she lacked the financial capital to get started. But she wasn't deterred. She got resourceful and asked her husband what they did with the old aluminum window frames they replaced at work. She learned that they were just sitting in a pile, collecting dust, so Susan got permission to break out the glass and recycle the aluminum for the cash she needed to fund her project.

She started small, and initially, the progress was

slow. Because she knew little about pricing or marketing, she again employed her knack for ingenuity to experiment and determine what worked. She hosted her products on Etsy and other websites designed to help creative people sell their handmade goods. If a product wasn't selling, she took that as negative feedback, tweaked the design, and tried uploading the product again. At the time, her bestselling product was a wallet priced at five dollars before shipping. She sold around 2,000 over a period of about two years. In the meantime, the couple welcomed another baby, this time a son, into the family, and this is when everything changed.

> **"Even though I didn't know what I was doing, and I still don't, I learned that I can set goals, and somehow, I'm able to reach them."**

When Susan couldn't find any "cute" shoes for her son, she decided to make her own. She hadn't ever made shoes before, so she went online, found a shoe pattern, and modified it to make what she had in mind: a simple pair of children's moccasins. She loved the finished result so much that she decided to put them online to see what her customers thought. They were a hit! Moccasins for babies became her staple product.

248   THE POWER OF STARTING SOMETHING STUPID

Sometime later, Susan received an e-mail from the fashion editor at *Parenting* magazine. The editor said she had been following Susan's story, loved the moccasins, and wanted Susan to send the magazine a pair as a gift for celebrity Kourtney Kardashian. Susan recalls, "I didn't know what to do. I didn't see what a big opportunity this was. In fact, I was kind of a brat." Essentially, Susan told the editor that if she wanted the moccasins, she'd have to pay for them just like everybody else. Luckily for Susan, the editor was patient with her lack of experience, and explained how editorials worked. Susan sent a pair of moccasins right away.

Kourtney Kardashian loved the moccasins and so did *Parenting* magazine. A picture of Kardashian's son wearing the moccasins landed on the magazine cover. And the week after the issue hit the shelves, Kourtney and her son were also seen in just about every gossip magazine—every time you saw the baby, you saw Susan's moccasins too!

Susan didn't know what to do with all the publicity she was receiving, so she asked a trusted friend in public relations for help. This friend referred her to an industry-specific publicist, and the rest is history. *Freshly Picked*, the leather goods shop Susan created to host her products online, is now a household name. Her products have been featured in *Parenting* magazine, *Us Weekly, In Touch, Good Housekeeping,* and more.

"Even though I didn't know what I was doing, and I still don't," Susan says, "I learned that I can set goals, and somehow, I'm able to reach them."

Defining Leverage

Leverage is the process of maximizing the resources that are available to us, in order to increase effectiveness. When we leverage, we aggregate and organize existing resources to achieve success.

Many high-potential ideas fail before they even move from stupid idea to project phase, because we become so fixated on the *lack* of resources we *think* we need for success (the Time-Education-Money Gap, for example). When this same energy is effectively channeled by ingenuity, we find ways to effectively leverage the resources we do, in fact, have available to us. Ironically, in so doing, we overcome the very circumstantial barriers we were fixating on in the first place.

Susan Petersen is the perfect example. Her story proves the proverbial saying "necessity is the mother of invention," and goes a step further to show how invention creates momentum and leads to meaningful results. Time and again, Susan was resourceful. She didn't fixate on lack; rather, she leveraged the resources available to her to overcome challenges and successfully meet her own needs. Susan leveraged existing resources to overcome the Time-Education-Money Gap.

Trying to implement your stupid idea without leveraging existing resources can be compared to trying to lift a car without using a jack. Leverage allows us to raise the car off the ground by simply turning a lever with one hand. There is still work required, and the process still takes time, but when effectively applied, leverage can increase the chance of success exponentially.

The Law of Leverage

The law of leverage is perhaps best illustrated by the story of Archimedes and King Hieron. Archimedes asserted to Hieron that given the proper execution, there was no weight he could not lift. He boldly proclaimed, "Give me a place to stand, and I shall move the Earth." Hieron retorted that it was easy to claim that which could not be proven. Hieron then challenged Archimedes to single-handedly move a large ship that "all the Syracusans with their combined strength were unable to launch."

At the appointed time, and in the presence of the king and many members of his kingdom, Archimedes "with no great endeavor but only holding the end of a compound pulley quietly in his hand and pulling at it, [drew] the ship along smoothly and safely as if she were moving through the seas." Hieron then declared that "from that day forth Archimedes was to be believed in everything he might say." By using leverage, Archimedes, with only one hand, was stronger and more effective than "all the Syracusans with their combined strength."

Leverage is nothing new. The concept is as old as time. Farmers leverage existing soil, seeds, and water to produce crops. Inventors leverage existing materials to produce new products. Manufacturers organize materials and design machines to produce other people's stupid ideas. Artists leverage existing materials to create art. Benjamin Franklin didn't invent electricity; he just leveraged it.

Think about your local supermarket. Do they actually produce *anything* they sell in the store? In some circumstances perhaps they do, but for the most part, your local supermarket leverages everyone else's existing products to stock their shelves with the food you put on your table. Movie theaters play movies made by other people, radio stations play music written by other people, and newspapers tell other people's stories. Teachers teach other people's information, and even authors often cite other authors to support the validity of their own claims.

Leveraging other people's information on the Internet is simply an online reflection of what has been happening for years in the physical world. Google Search can be effectively summed up in one word: leverage. It is built entirely on leveraging other people's information. Google

Search didn't create the information it provides, just the tool that organizes it. The same goes for Facebook, YouTube, Twitter, Wikipedia, Amazon, and other big Internet guys. They are the great aggregators. They provide the platform; you provide the content. They add value to our world with a tool, and we allow them to leverage our information to grow. Everyone wins.

> "Individually, we are one drop. Together, we are an ocean."
> —RYUNOSUKE SATORO, JAPANESE POET

And yet, we balk at the idea of leverage. We shy away from leverage for the same myriad of reasons we don't readily overcome our pride, ask for what we need, receive from others, or extend trust. We tell ourselves that if our success isn't built independently, from the ground up, it is somehow less respectable. Let me ask you, if a farmer doesn't lay his own eggs, is he really a fraud?

If you are convinced that the only way to respectably succeed is on your own, you will never achieve your highest potential for success.

Hiding in Plain Sight:
Identifying the Levers in Your Life

All the resources you need are *already* at your disposal. Attempting to succeed without embracing the tools immediately available for your success is no less absurd than trying to row a boat by drawing only your hands through the water or trying to unscrew a screw using nothing more than your fingernail. There are levers all around us, hiding in plain sight. Find them. Use them. The following are a few ways to leverage existing resources to overcome the challenges you face.

Leverage Existing Technology

Advances in technology have given us the amazing ability to influence and be influenced on a vast and immeasurable scale. Virtually anything is possible with the information, tools, and services available to us on the Internet.

In a matter of only hours, you could launch your own TV show (YouTube, Vimeo), publish your own book (Amazon), start a newspaper column (blog), or open an international marketplace (website). You could hire a virtual assistant from the dinner table and outsource manufacturing without getting up from the couch. By leveraging technology, you can even develop meaningful relationships and instantly market your products and ideas to relevant demographics by utilizing existing social media platforms.

For example, when I wrote *Résumés Are Dead and What to Do About It,* I had no idea how to design an e-book. I wrote the content, and then I was stuck. I wanted to present the book in a way that was fresh, engaging, and artistic, but the problem was I only had five days to complete it in time to give it away at an upcoming speech. So, naturally, I used technology to solve my problem.

I went online to Guru.com and eLance.com (websites where you can search for freelancers), and people from all over the world submitted bids to design the book. Within hours, I had hired a graphic designer from the Ukraine! The book was completed in time, the response was fantastic, and my publisher ended up picking up the book and republishing it under their label. After the official launch on Amazon, *Résumés Are Dead and What to Do About It* hit #1 on the Business and Investing list, #1 in Careers, #1 in Job Hunting and broke the Top 100 of all free Kindle books. When you combine the power of starting something stupid with the unstoppable force of leverage, what you get is magic.

A quick word of warning about technology:

Beware the technological tattoo.

The content you post online is published and potentially searchable forever. Reckless use of social media sites and other online resources can result in lasting negative effects.

At any time, your current or future employer, school admissions board, or spouse could look up anything you've ever posted. Do you really want your high-school or college drama haunting you when you're in your fifties?

Approach life with the highest standards of integrity, authenticity, and forethought, even—and especially—on the playground of the World Wide Web.

Leverage Ties

Strong Ties. To achieve your goals, it's essential to develop strong ties by developing genuine relationships with good, like-minded (and better-minded) friends and associates. Friends tend to think, act, and even dress alike. You will be inspired, motivated, and even shaped by the attributes of the people you spend the greatest amount of time with. By associating with good people who share your same vision, you (and they) are perfectly positioned to collaborate and leverage one another's unique talents and assets effectively should the opportunity arise.

Remove yourself from negative people and situations. You'll be more effective in the long run. It's been said, "One bad apple can spoil the whole barrel." When you associate with people who hold themselves to a lower standard of performance, don't exercise the highest level of integrity, and/or don't engage in abundance thinking,

over time your own effectiveness, integrity, and core beliefs about success will begin to shift as well. As some
say, "If you want to be a millionaire, hang around with
millionaires," so it is with any endeavor. If you want to
move mountains and make meaningful waves, hang out
with mountain movers and wave makers. Your power to
effectively lead and accomplish dreams will increase.

Weak Ties. Our strong ties help us gain access to
what professor Mark Granovetter describes as "weak
ties." In their book, *Being the Boss: The 3 Imperatives for
Becoming a Great Leader,* Harvard professor Linda Hill
and business executive Kent Lineback further develop
Granovetter's concept stating, "Weak ties . . . connect
you with worlds different from your own and extend your
reach to provide access to unique information and other
resources."

   The concept of weak ties can be likened to the
popular theory of "the six degrees of separation." In essence, this theory maintains that through other connections, each person is never more than approximately six
connections away from any other person or resource on
Earth. If you don't have direct access to a person or resource you need to achieve your goal, chances are good
that you can leverage one of your strong ties to ultimately
connect with the resources you need. For example, I
leveraged the power of ties (both strong and weak) and

combined it with the power of START to engage and connect with the bestselling authors who reviewed and endorsed this book.

Leverage Time

Ultimately the reason leverage is so vitally important is because it helps us effectively manage our time. Remember the lessons learned in Gavin's Law. Life is short. We have a limited and undetermined amount of time available to achieve our goals. This limited resource is passing by no matter what. Leverage time and make it effectively work to your advantage.

Abundance of Time. If you don't have all the resources you need to succeed, but you do have an abundance of free time available to you, you can effectively leverage that time to help you achieve your goals. Leverage free time by researching ideas, making meaningful connections, or studying the success of others in the same field you want to pursue. Don't waste the endless possibilities provided by discretionary time.

Lack of Time. When you lack available time, you can leverage the time (and thus other useful resources) of others through collaboration. Often, when we *do* have time available to work toward our goals, we aren't as prone to call on the expertise or resources of other people. In this way, lack of time can be a blessing, as it requires us to leverage other people's time, and thus their unique talents, to achieve success.

If you lack time, actively seek out partnerships, collaboration, and opportunities to outsource. As the saying goes, "many hands make light work." We maximize success both in terms of reach and acceleration when we leverage other people's time and talents to achieve greater success.

Leverage Education and/or Experience

Find a Mentor. If you don't have the education and/or experience you need to reach success, you can overcome learning curves by working with a mentor. Mentors already have the knowledge, experience, and skill necessary to make things happen. There is no reason to unnecessarily repeat the same mistakes others have already made. When you leverage these relationships, you stand on the shoulders of giants and achieve things far greater than either of you ever could have done on your own.

For example, Bill Hewlett, cofounder of Hewlett-Packard Company (HP), mentored young Steve Jobs. When Jobs was only in the eighth grade, he needed parts for a school project.

Someone suggested that he call Bill Hewlett. Finding a William Hewlett in the telephone book, the 12-year-old Jobs called and asked, "Is this the Bill Hewlett of

Hewlett-Packard?" "Yes," said Bill. Jobs made his request. Bill spent some time talking to him about his project. Several days later, Jobs went to HP and picked up a bag full of parts that Bill had put together for him. Subsequently, Jobs landed a summer job at HP.

Mentors don't have to be people you meet in person. Some of my greatest mentors died hundreds of years ago. Read books and biographies to leverage the experience and wisdom of others. Leaders are readers. There's a reason for that. The more you read, the more effectively you'll lead. I'm constantly seeking out mentors—in real life and through books—to help me overcome learning curves and achieve my personal goals.

Be a Mentor. Leverage your education and experience by being a mentor. Mentoring others allows us to be involved in projects that for a myriad of reasons we might otherwise not have access to. Maybe age and declining health are keeping us from being involved in certain projects, or perhaps success in other areas leaves us with a lack of time leftover for other things. Whatever the reason, becoming a mentor allows us to still contribute in meaningful ways to projects we are passionate about. Your protégé will love the experience and knowledge you bring to the table, and you'll have eager and energetic hands to do the work you'd otherwise be unable to perform.

Among others, Steve Jobs mentored Google co-founder Larry Page and Facebook's Mark Zuckerberg. Of mentoring others Jobs said,

> That's how I'm going to spend part of the time I have left. I can help the next generation remember the lineage of great companies here and how to continue the tradition. The Valley has been very supportive of me. I should do my best to repay.

Being a mentor is a wonderful way to "pay it forward" and make your mark on the future.

Leverage Money

Money may not make the world go round, but it sure makes some things a heck of a lot easier.

Lack of Money. Lack of money can be one of the most debilitating psychological hurdles to overcome when trying to get your ideas off the ground. To overcome this psychological barrier, it is often helpful to put things in perspective.

Half of the world's population lives on less than two dollars a day. If you are reading this book, it's highly probable that you are living above the average global income. Lack of money is all relative, right? When we change our psychology and recognize how advantaged we truly are, we are more readily able to recognize the resources immediately available to us that we simply do not currently recognize as such.

When we lack money, we leverage our ingenuity to eventually achieve success. Susan Petersen's ultimate success with her leather goods company is a prime example. When she didn't have the money to buy the materials she needed to start her project, she got creative and broke the glass out of discarded aluminum window frames in order to recycle the metal for cash. That's leverage! You can leverage your creativity to obtain the capital you seek.

Do as much as you can on your own without money. Leverage your lack of money as an opportunity to perform due diligence in preparation to start effectively when you do have the funds you need. Map your project out. Determine the foundational work that needs to be done in order to get your idea off the ground. Partner with and/or get help fundraising with someone who has the resources you lack. People are much more likely to invest in your ideas if you've already put in the blood, sweat, and tears to lay a solid foundation for success. Chances are there is plenty of initial work that doesn't require capital. Just get going!

Be optimistic. Think as if everything is going to magically come together in your behalf, and then work as if your life depended on it. That's how Natalie and I have done it. As entrepreneurs, we've experienced times of both feast and famine. In times of famine, we've found that remaining positive, sticking together, and working like there is no tomorrow is an effective formula for weathering nearly any storm—even if that meant recycling cans for cash to get us by while we worked toward our dreams.

Enough Money. If you're fortunate enough to have the money to fuel your project on your own, *be grateful.* Still actively perform due diligence and then leverage your resources wisely and conservatively to ensure your money goes as far as it possibly can.

Leverage: Drawing from the Well Called START

You have to dig a well before you can draw water from it. When we authentically live the principles of START, we dig the well. When we leverage, we draw from it. By genuinely living the principles of START, you ensure that you always have a deep well to draw from when the need inevitably arises. In essence, by STARTing, you're laying groundwork to effectively spur a groundswell when the time is right.

Unfortunately, many people think, and even teach, that the way to leverage is through networking. While networking is helpful, it can only get you so far—especially when you think networking equates to going to a conference, using gimmicky conversation starters, and handing out as many business cards as possible. That type of networking is "a mile wide and an inch deep." To create the type of results you need to succeed, you have to go much, much deeper.

It has been taught time and time again that to be successful you need other people to help propel you farther than you could ever go on your own. Bestselling author John C. Maxwell taught about how to get results with what he calls "The Law of the Inner Circle." Maxwell says, "Nobody does anything great alone. . . . What makes the difference is the leader's inner circle. Inner circle members should also add value to you personally. That's not selfish. If they have a negative effect, they will hinder your ability to lead well." Maxwell explains that inner circle members should "display excellence, maturity, and good character in everything they do." I would add to Maxwell's thought and emphasize the vital importance of you as an individual working to "display excellence, maturity, and good character in everything [you] do." This ensures you have a surplus of reciprocal trust to leverage should the need arise. Living the principles of START in every aspect of our lives ensures we consciously develop a surplus of trust and a strong, reliable inner circle.

If you assume you can "use" other people to get what

you want, you've completely misunderstood the principle of leverage. If you abuse the power of leverage, you'll burn bridges and miss out on creating sustainable success. START embodies abundance thinking. It is founded on the principle that there is enough to go around. Leverage, when employed from the foundation of START, is not only how we reach our own high aspirations. Through START we are also available to be leveraged by others to help them reach their highest potential for success as well. When leverage draws from the well of START, everyone wins.

The Lever That Moves the World

When you truly understand leverage, you know that you already have everything you need to achieve success. Paradoxically, that's often why it's so hard to start.

Muhammad Yunas, the father of microlending, leveraged the twenty-seven dollars he had in his pocket and eventually established a system of microloans that changed the lives of countless people the world over. In speaking to a group of college students, he was asked this question: "There are so many things that concern me, so many problems that need working on. . . . Where do you think I should start?" Yunas replied: "Start with whatever is right in front of you. Start with whatever is within your reach. That's how I got started. With one woman who needed a little bit of money to get out from underneath a loan shark."

Even your smallest efforts can spark great changes. Start by leveraging the resources that are most accessible to you.

Leverage is not just a principle of personal success. Leverage is truly a principle that can change the world, and without your contribution, the world will be less than it otherwise could be.

> *"We feel what we are doing is just a drop in the ocean, but that ocean would be less without that drop."*
> —MOTHER TERESA

There is a Polish proverb that says, "If each person would sweep before his own house, the city would soon be clean." Imagine how the earth could change overnight if everyone chose to embrace the New Smart, live dreams, and spur positive change right outside his or her own front door. When we leverage the resources available to us in meaningful ways, we can change the world for good and achieve greater happiness and success along the way.

LIVE WITHOUT REGRET

14

The End of the Book.
The Beginning of Your New Smart Life

"Never give up on something that you can't
go a day without thinking about."
—Unknown

The milk was sour.

I was standing in the middle of Ulaanbaatar, halfway around the world, politely sipping fermented mare's milk. We'd just finished meeting with the landlord of the building we rented for our cashmere company, and the horse milk was a celebratory gesture from my Mongolian business partner, Odgo.

In my wildest of dreams, I never imagined that my stupid idea to help people in developing countries become self-reliant through self-employment would lead me here, to Outer Mongolia. In the end, the company didn't work out the way we had planned, but this failed project started me down a path toward some of the most amazing opportunities of my life thus far. One thing led to another, in truly miraculous ways.

My life has been a series of leaning into some seriously stupid ideas. Time and time again, I've experienced the very real power of starting something stupid . . . and I'm hooked.

While interviewing hundreds of people in the sunset of their lives, I heard the same laments over and over again. Regrets like, "I wish I'd taken that big trip," "I wish I'd followed through on that idea," "I wish I'd pursued my dreams." I heard it all. But in nearly every case, the biggest regret I heard was, "I wish I'd spent more time with the people I love. I wish I'd spent more time with my family."

What if I had been too distracted by the busyness of life to make room in my schedule to be a good dad? What if I had been too prideful to change a diaper? What if I had given in to procrastination and convinced myself I'd have more time to hang out with my boys later, *after* I had built a successful career?

Thankfully, I was stupid enough to spend every moment I could with my sons, or I'd share that tragic lament of "I wish. . . ."

Your life should consist of more than commuting, working, eating, surfing the Internet, sleeping, and watching TV. Your life should be filled with purpose-driven experiences and projects that bring excitement, passion, energy, and authentic meaning and joy into your life. I hope that as you start something stupid, you will find real meaning in your life and that you will learn these three great (albeit simple) truths:

1. Your life matters.
2. Your life has purpose.
3. You are meant to be happy.

May this book be a source of inspiration for some of the coolest and most meaningful projects and experiences of your life! It all starts with a tiny, stupid idea, then one thing leads to another, and suddenly, you find something amazing: yourself.

Additional Resources

Bonus! The 76-Day Challenge

I've developed an action guide called the 76-Day Challenge. You can access your free guide at www.Richie Norton.com/76DayChallenge. Also available is a free excerpt of *Résumés Are Dead and What to Do About It.*

Access to Free Resources and More

Website: www.RichieNorton.com

Blog: www.RichieNorton.com/Blog

Subscribe: www.RichieNorton.com/email-subscribe

Social Media Connections

Facebook: www.Facebook.com/RichieNorton

Twitter: www.Twitter.com/RichieNorton

LinkedIn: www.LinkedIn.com/in/RichardNorton
   #powerofstupid and #newsmart

Contact, Speaking, or Consulting Inquiries

E-mail: Richie@RichieNorton.com

Acknowledgments

Writing a book is work—hard work. You know this will be the case going in, but you can't possibly imagine just how hard it's really going to get until you're up to your neck in the process (and by then it begins to feel suspiciously like a noose). To all who helped me bring this book to life, please know that no expression of thanks will ever be a sufficient representation of the depth of gratitude I feel.

First, to my beautiful wife, Natalie, who came to my rescue through countless long days and dozens of sleepless nights and helped me translate my thoughts and research into graceful, relevant, readable art. (I love you, Nat!) To my remarkable children for their unconditional love and patience. To my amazing parents, grandparents and parents-in-law for their unyielding support, selfless sacrifice, and ceaseless encouragement. To my brother, sisters, their spouses and each of my nieces and nephews for being such an inspiration to me. Family is everything, and mine is the best.

To two of my heroes, Sheri Dew and Chris Schoebinger, for first believing in me and this book project and for welcoming me into the Shadow Mountain Publishing family with such conviction and enthusiasm. To my editors, Lisa Mangum and Leslie Stitt for their truly angelic patience, persistence, and precision. To Gail Halladay, Richard Erickson, Brad Haslam, Dallas Petersen, Scott Christley, Dave Kimball, Mike Jensen, Chrislyn Barnes Woolston, Erin Hallstrom, Lee Broadhead, John Rose, Lonnie Lockhart, Sonia Larson, and the whole Shadow Mountain team for catching the vision behind the message, and for going the extra mile (or ten) to make this book a success.

To the vastly talented Erin Jane Riley for breathing life into this project through her amazing art. To Barry Hansen for designing the models with such acute attention to detail. To Rachael Ward for slaying the typesetting dragon and presenting these words with elegance.

To the late Dr. Stephen R. Covey for being a supreme example and mentor. To Stephen M. R. Covey for taking me under his wing with such gracious and genuine care. To Seth Godin for leading the way. To Jack Canfield for guiding me through "breakthrough" experiences. To Andy Andrews for teaching me the behind-the-scenes realities of writing and presenting. To Devin Graham for inspiring me with his fierce dedication to making dreams happen. To Chris Bennett for his loyalty and wise guidance. To Jase Bennett for his treasured example and friendship, and for being such a willing and valuable sounding board. To Dal Zemp for taking a chance on me.

To all those who believed in this message (and in me) and took the precious time to endorse and promote this book. In particular, thanks to my unbelievable father-in-law, Greg Link. Greg, I am absolutely humbled by your contribution.

To the hundreds of individuals I interviewed over the years who offered me such an intimate and authentic look into their lives—this book would not exist without each of you.

And of course, thanks to you, the reader, for taking the message of this book and running with it. You thrill me to no end!

Most of all, I thank my loving Father in Heaven for all the blessings, purpose, potential, and joy this life has to offer.

Notes

PART I

Page 3 "Stay hungry." See http://news.stanford.edu/news/2005 /june15/jobs-061505.html.

Page 3 "The difference between genius" Attributed to Albert Einstein, as quoted in John William Gardener, *Sharing Leadership Tasks* (New York: Free Press, 1990), 151.

Page 3 "First he told me" Pierre Omidyar, as quoted in Alyson Shontell, "10 Super Successful Cofounders and Why Their Partners Worked," *Business Insider,* June 4, 2011.

Page 3 "A lot of people" Biz Stone, as quoted in "How Biz Stone Became a Mighty Force on the Internet and Co-founded Twitter," Woculus: first-class info for business, woculus.com/tag /biz-stone.

Page 3 "Everything I do" Author interview with Seth Godin, January 11, 2011.

Page 3 "We don't like their sound" Quoted in Steven Rogers and Roza Makonnen, *The Entrepreneur's Guide to Finance and Business Wealth Creation Techniques for Growing a Business* (New York: McGraw-Hill, 2003), 41.

Page 4 "Are you crazy?" Paul Newman, as quoted in Doug Dvorak, *Build Your Own Brand* (Gretna, Louisiana: Pelican Publishing, 2010), 19.

Page 4 "When I proposed" David Neeleman, as quoted in Edward M. Hallowell, "Overloaded Circuits: Why Smart People

Underperform," *Harvard Business Review on Bringing Your Whole Self to Work* (Boston: Harvard Business School Publishing, 2008), 6.

Page 4 "We allow no geniuses" Walt Disney, as quoted in Derek Walter, *Animated Architecture* (New York: St. Martins, 1982), 10.

Page 4 "The fool doth think" William Shakespeare, *As You Like It*, 5.1.30–31.

Page 4 "Here's to the crazy ones" Peter Diamandis and Steven Kotter, *Abundance: The Future Is Better Than You Think* (New York: Free Press, 2012), 232.

CHAPTER 1

Page 10 "Don't be fooled" Charles Dow Richards, as quoted in Richard Scott, *I Don't Have Time* (Croydon, Surrey: Filament Publishing, 2010), 40. Original quotation states "in the year."

Page 15 "Everything can be taken" Viktor E. Frankl, *Man's Search for Meaning* (New York: Pocket Books, 1959), 86.

CHAPTER 2

Page 17 "In every work of genius" Ralph Waldo Emerson and Edward Waldo Emerson, *The Complete Works of Ralph Waldo Emerson* (Boston and New York: The Riverside Press, Cambridge, 1904), 45.

Page 17 "All of a sudden" Author interview with Clay Leavitt, May–July 2012.

Page 23 "par·a·dox" http://oxforddictionaries.com/definition/english /paradox.

Page 23 "a culturematic is a little machine" Grant McCracken, *Culturematic: How Reality TV, John Cheever, a Pie Lab, Julia Child, Fantasy Football, Burning Man, the Ford Fiesta Movement, Rube Goldberg, NFL Films, Wordle, Two and a Half Men, a 10,000-Year Symphony and ROFLCon Memes Will Help You*

Create and Execute Breakthrough Ideas (Boston: Harvard Business School Publishing, 2012), 3.

Page 23 "The paradox" See http://blogs.hbr.org/ideacast/2012/05 /make-your-own-culturematic.html.

Page 25 "Doggles" See "Surprising Ideas That Made Millions," CNBC, n.d., http://www.cnbc.com/id/46747902/Surprising _Ideas_That%20Made_Millions?slide=2.

Page 26 "Chia Pets" See "Chia Pet," Smithsonian, n.d., http://www .smithsonianmag.com/arts-culture/object-chiapet-200712.html.

Page 26 "Angry Birds" See "Rovio Entertainment Reports 2011 Financial Results," Rovio, July 5, 2012, http://www.rovio.com /en/news/press-releases/161/rovio-entertainment-reports-2011 -financial-results/.

Page 26 "[I] approached several lawyers" "Sara's Story," See http:// www.spanx.com/corp/index.jsp?page=sarasStory&clickId =sarasstory_aboutsara_text.

Page 26 "they all thought" Wes Moss, *Starting from Scratch: Secrets from 22 Ordinary People Who Made the Entrepreneurial Leap* (New York: Kaplan Publishing, 2008), 81.

Page 26 "'stupid' and 'wouldn't sell'" See "Sara's Story."

Page 26 "I received a call" Ibid.

Page 27 "The device is inherently" Clifford Pickover, "Traveling Through Time," Nova Online, October 12, 1999, http://www .pbs.org/wgbh/nova/time/through2.html.

Page 27 "The horse is here to stay" Jeff Siegel, Chris Nelder, and Nick Hodge, *Investing in Renewable Energy: Making Money on Green Chip Stocks* (Hoboken, NJ: John Wiley & Sons Inc., 2008), 612.

Page 27 "The wireless music box" Wai Mun Chia and Hui Ying Sng, eds., *Singapore and Asia in a Globalized World: Contemporary Economic Issues and Policies* (Singapore: World Publishing, 2009), 29.

Page 28 "A man-made moon voyage" Lee De Forest, as quoted in

"De Forest Says Space Travel Is Impossible," *Lewiston Morning Tribune* via Associated Press, February 25, 1957.

Page 28 "There is practically no chance" T. Craven, as quoted in Niall Edworthy and Petra Cramsie, *The Optimist's/Pessimist's Handbook: A Companion to Hope and Despair* (New York, NY: Free Press, 2008), 68.

Page 28 "I don't know now" Thomas Edison, as quoted in Sarah Knowles Bolton, *Poor Boys Who Became Famous* (New York: Thomas Y. Crowell, 1922), 360–61.

Page 28 "he lacked imagination" Walt Disney, as quoted in Richard Keith Latman, *The Good Fail: Entrepreneurial Lessons from the Rise and Fall of Mocroworkz* (Hoboken, NJ: John Wiley & Sons, Inc., 2012), 141.

Page 28 "You ain't goin' nowhere" Jimmy Denny, as quoted in Ken McFarland, *I Don't See It That Way: It Looks a Little Different from Up Here* (Hagerstown, MD: Review and Herald Publishing Association, 2009), 71.

Page 29 "Whenever you see" Peter Drucker, as quoted in Peter Archer, *The Quotable Intellectual: 1,417 Bon Mots, Ripostes, and Witticisims for Aspiring Academics, Armchair Philosophers and Anyone Else Who Wants to Sound Really Smart* (Avon, MA: Adams Media, 2010), 190.

Page 30 "I could give you" Jack Welch and Suzy Welch, *Winning* (New York, NY: HarperCollins, 2005), 71.

CHAPTER 3

Page 35 "I plead with you" Thomas S. Monson, "Finding Joy in the Journey," *Ensign*, November 2008, 85.

Page 36 "How much of human life" Ralph Waldo Emerson, *Emerson: Essays and Lectures: Nature: Addresses and Lectures/ Essays: First and Second Series/Representative Men/English Traits/ The Conduct of Life (Library of America)* (New York: Penguin Putnam, 1983), 364.

Page 37 *The Monk and the Riddle* See http://www.kpcb.com/partner/randy-komisar.

Page 37 "Step one" Randy Komisar, *The Monk and the Riddle: The Education of a Silicon Valley Entrepreneur* (Boston: Harvard Business Review Press, 2001), 65.

Page 37 "getting rich fast" Ibid., 65–66. See also 149, 155.

Page 37 "For a long time" Alfred D'Souza, as quoted in Skip Downing, *On Course Strategies for Creating Success in College and in Life* (Boston: Wadsworth, 2011), 9.

Page 38 "It's incredibly easy" Stephen R. Covey, *The 7 Habits of Highly Effective People* (New York: Free Press, 1989, 2004), 98.

Page 38 "Begin with the end" Ibid.

Page 38 "When it's time to die" Henry David Thoreau, as quoted in Richard Scott, *I Don't Have Time* (Croydon, Surrey: Filament Publishing, 2010), 105.

Page 38 "The vast majority" Komisar, 65–66.

Page 41 "Often they put a restriction" "Germany became the first nation in the world to adopt an old-age social insurance program in 1889, designed by Germany's Chancellor, Otto von Bismarck." "History," Social Security Online, http://www.ssa.gov/history/age65.html. In 1884, the Baltimore and Ohio Railroad established one of the first major retirement plans, which allowed workers who had worked for the railroad for at least ten years to retire and receive benefits at age sixty-five. See Elizabeth Fee, Linda Shopes, and Linda Zeidman, *The Baltimore Book: New Views of Local History* (Philadelphia: Temple University Press, 1991), 11. The Pension Act of 1890 made it so all veterans age sixty-five and older who had served more than ninety days and were honorably discharged could receive a regular payment without working. See Steven Green Livingston, *United States Social Security: A Reference Handbook* (Santa Barbara, CA: ABC-CLIO, 2008), 115.

Page 41 "several generations" In 2010, the US Social Security

Administration paid about 59.2 million people social security benefits. See http://www.ssa.gov/policy/docs/chartbooks/fast _facts/2011/fast_facts11.html#highlights.

Page 42 "How do your decisions" http://www.fourhourwork week.com/blog/about/.

Page 42 "Don't ever confuse" Quindlen commencement address, Villanova, June 23, 2000. http://www.cs.oswego.edu/~wender /quindlen.html.

Page 44 "Good things may come" Attributed to Abraham Lincoln, as quoted in Paul W. Bush, Stuart G. Walesh, *Managing and Leading: 44 Lessons Learned for Pharmacists* (Bethesda, MD: American Society of Health-System Pharmacists, 2004), 54.

Page 45 "So what do we" Lee Iacocca, in John Cook, *The Book of Positive Quotations* (Minneapolis, MN: Rubicon Press, Inc., 1993), 315.

CHAPTER 4

Page 49 "Do not act" Marcus Aurelius Antoninus, Emperor of Rome, translated by George Long, *Meditations*, (Sioux Falls, SD: NuVision Publications, 2008), 27.

Page 49 "When I'm eighty" See Josepha Sherman, *Jeff Bezos: King of Amazon* (New York: Twenty-First Century Books, 2001), 25.

Page 50 "I went to my boss" "Jeffrey P. Bezos," interview, American Academy of Achievement, May 4, 2001, http://www.achievement .org/autodoc/page/bez0int-3.

Page 51 "If you can project yourself" Ibid.

Page 52 "Person of the Year" See *Time*, December 27, 1999; see also "Jeffrey P. Bezos," interview.

Page 52 "It is not the critic" Theodore Roosevelt, "Citizenship in a Republic," speech at the Sorbonne, Paris, April 23, 1910, as quoted in Donald J. Davidson, *The Wisdom of Theodore Roosevelt* (New York: Kensington Publishing, 2003), 48.

Page 56 "The common question" Jeff Bezos, as quoted in http://www.wired.com/magazine/2011/11/ff_bezos/all/1.

Page 59 "If at first" Attributed to Albert Einstein, as quoted in Conrad P. Pritscher, *Einstein & Zen: Learning to Learn* (New York, NY: Peter Lang Publishing, 2010), 57.

CHAPTER 5

Page 63 "Do what you can" Theodore Roosevelt, quoted in James M. Strock, *Theodore Roosevelt on Leadership: Executive Lessons from the Bully Pulpit*, 2003, Google e-book, chapter 1.

Page 63 "There was no funding" Simon Sinek, *Start With Why: How Great Leaders Inspire Everyone to Take Action* (New York: Penguin Books, 2009), 2.

Page 64 "The public can call us" Orville and Wilbur Wright, as quoted in James Tobin, *To Conquer the Air: The Wright Brothers and the Great Race for Flight* (New York: Free Press, 2008), 146; see also Peter Jakab and Rick Young, eds., *The Published Writings of Wilbur and Orville Wright* (New York: Random House, 2004), 275.

Page 66 "A year from now" Karen Lamb, as quoted in Rodolfo Costa, *Advice My Parents Gave Me: And Other Lessons I Learned from My Mistakes*, 2011, Google e-book, chapter 2.

Page 68 "Work expands" Edward E. Zajac, *Political Economy of Fairness* (Cambridge, MA: MIT Press, 2001), 50.

Page 70 "On the individual level" Stephen M. R. Covey, *The Speed of Trust: The One Thing That Changes Everything* (New York: Free Press, 2006), 102.

Page 71 "Experience is the opposite" Paul Arden, *It's Not How Good You Are, It's How Good You Want to Be* (New York: Phaidon Press, 2003), 54.

Page 72 "All of this meaning" Author interview with Anna Hargadon, June 11, 2012.

Page 72 "Oprah was born" See Nicole Mowbray, "Oprah's Path to Power," *The Observer,* March 2, 2003.

Page 72 "Today, she is one" See Clare O'Connor, "Forbes 400: Meet America's Richest Women (And Not Just Oprah and Meg)," *Forbes,* September 22, 2011; http://www.forbes.com/sites/clareoconnor/2011/09/22/forbes-400-meet-americas-richest-women-and-not-just-oprah-and-meg/.

Page 72 "J.K. Rowling went" William A. McEachern, *Contemporary Economics* (Mason, OH: Southwestern, Cengage Learning, 2008), 11.

Page 72 "Rock bottom became" J.K. Rowling, Harvard University commencement address, June 5, 2008, http://vimeo.com/1711302.

Page 73 "Steve Jobs felt guilty" "'You've Got to Find What You Love,' Jobs says," *Stanford University News,* June 14, 2005, http://news.stanford.edu/news/2005/june15/jobs-061505.html.

Page 73 "the most valuable company" See "10 Most Valuable Companies in America: Wall St. 24/7," Huff Post Business, August 10, 2011, http://www.huffingtonpost.com/2011/08/10/ten-most-valuable-companies-america_n_923752.html#s326803&title=10_Procter. See http://www.forbes.com/sites/davidthier/2012/08/20/apple-becomes-the-most-valuable-company-of-all-time/.

Page 75 "*People* magazine reported" James S. Kunen, "Pop! Goes the Donald," *People,* July 9, 1990, http://www.people.com/people/archive/article/0,,20118158,00.html.

PART III

Page 79 "Creative leaders invite" IBM, *Capitalizing on Complexity: Insights from the Global Executive Officer Study* (Somers, NY: IBM Corporation, 2010), 10.

CHAPTER 6

Page 83 "Business men go down" Henry Ford and Samuel Crowther, *My Life and Work* (Garden City, NY: Garden City Publishing Co., Inc., 1922), 43.

Page 83 "And whenever Henry stopped" Don Mitchell, *Driven: A Photobiography of Henry Ford* (New York: National Geographic Books, 2010), 16.

Page 84 "Ford's Model T" See Forbes Sample Material, 2006 (New York: John Wiley & Sons, Inc., 1996), http://www.wiley.com /legacy/products/subject/business/forbes/ford.html.

Page 84 "half of all cars" See John Farndon, *DK Eyewitness Books: Oil* (New York: DK Publishing, 2012), 14.·

Page 84 "Many men are afraid" Ibid., 44.

Page 84 "This more than doubled" David A. Hounshell, *From the American System to Mass Production, 1800–1932* (Baltimore, MD: Johns Hopkins University Press, 1985), 289.

Page 84 "Ford was hailed" Daniel Gross, *Forbes Greatest Business Stories of All Time* (Hoboken, NJ: John Wiley & Sons, Inc., 1996), 83–84.

Page 84 "Stockholders considered him" Ibid.

Page 84 "His innovation proved successful" Hounshell, *American System*, 289.

Page 84 "The payment of five dollars" "Building a car for the Great Multitude," Forbes Sample Material, *Forbes* (New York: John Wiley & Sons, Inc., 1996), n.p., http://www.wiley.com /legacy/products/subject/business/forbes/ford.html.

Page 85 "The market began to shift" "The Model T's Ride Comes to an End," Forbes Sample Material, n.d., http://www.wiley .com/legacy/products/subject/business/forbes/ford.html; see also Gross, 86.

Page 87 "requires the activity" James F. Welles, *Understanding Stupidity*, n.d., www.stupidity.net/story2/index2.htm.

Page 89 "we all live in 'permanent beta'" Reid Hoffman and Ben

Cosnocha, *The Start-up of YOU: Adapt to the Future, Invest in Yourself and Transform Your Career* (New York: Crown Publishing, 2012), 21–22, 225.

Page 89 "make uncertainty" Ibid.

Page 89 "mind-set brimming" Ibid., 21–22.

Page 89 "Web 2.0 applications" IAN, "10 definitions of Web 2.0 and their shortcomings," August 17, 2006.

Page 89 "Permanent beta" Hoffman and Cosnocha, 22.

Page 90 "planned obsolescence" "Case Study: GM and the Great Automation Solution," *Why Smart Executives Fail*, n.d., http://mba.tuck.dartmouth.edu/pages/faculty/syd.finkelstein/case_studies/01.html; see also Alfred Pritchard Sloan, *My Years with General Motors* (New York: Crown Business, 1990), 167–68.

Page 90 "By 1926, T sales" "The Model T's Ride."

Page 91 "was a success" Ibid.

CHAPTER 7

Page 93 "All life is an experiment" Ralph Waldo Emerson et al., *Journals of Ralph Waldo Emerson: With Annotations*, Vol. 6 (Boston and New York: Houghton Mifflin Company, 1911), 302.

Page 94 "I quickly discovered" See http://www.problogger.net/archives/2006/01/25/becoming-a-problogger/.

Page 96 "Rowse's network of blogs" See http://www.adweek.com/news/technology/alloy-digital-acquires-b5media-139733.

Page 96 "Problogger.net" See http://technorati.com/blogs/www.problogger.net.

Page 96 "Digital-Photography-School.com" See http://digital-photography-school.com/advertise-on-digital-photography-school.

Page 98 "how personal projects" Book description of Brian R. Little et al., eds., *Personal Project Pursuit: Goals, Action and Human Flourishing*, Amazon.com, n.d., http://www.amazon.com/Personal-Project-Pursuit-Action-Flourishing/dp/080585486X.

Page 98 "In the final analysis" Brian R. Little et al., *Personal Projects and Organizational Lives* (Mahwah, NJ: Lawrence Erlbaum, 2007), 221–222, 239; http://www.management.wharton.upenn.edu/grant/GrantLittlePhillipsPPP.pdf.

Page 101 "to find, foster, and fund" See http://cainesarcade.com/thefoundation/; See also http://www.youtube.com/watch?v=faIFNkdq96U.

Page 101 "Caine also received" See http://cainesarcade.com/about/; See also http://www.canneslions.com/the_festival/speakers/inc_speaker.cfm?speaker_id=302.

Page 101 "This has opened" See http://www.nerdist.com/2012/04/interview-the-creator-of-caines-arcade-has-his-perfect-moment/.

Page 103 "Just start something" Author interview with Chris Bennett, June 14, 2012.

Page 104 "A lot of people think" "Creating Innovation at the Office," Trend Hunter Keynotes, January 2012, YouTube video, http://www.trendhunter.com/keynote/mark-zuckerberg.

Page 105 "We offer our engineers" "The Engineer's Life at Google," Google, http://www.google.com/intl/FR_be/jobs/lifeatgoogle/englife/index.html.

Page 107 "How do you start" Author interview with Lara Casey, July 20, 2012.

Page 109 "the greatest commercial" See http://www.macobserver.com/news/99/june/990629/tvguide1984.html.

Page 109 "Well, I'll pay half" Walter Isaacson, *Steve Jobs* (New York, NY: Simon & Schuster, 2011), 164.

Page 111 "A pessimist sees" Winston Churchill, in Richard Langworth, *Churchill By Himself: The Definitive Collection of Quotations* (London, UK: Ebury Press, 2008), 578.

PART IV

Page 113 "the foundation for a system" See http://oxforddictionaries.com/definition/english/principle.

Page 114 "The Latin root for *principles*" Ibid.

Page 117 "All our dreams" Walt Disney, in Pat Williams, James Denney, Jim Denney, *How to Be Like Walt: Capturing the Disney Magic Every Day of Your Life* (Deerfield Beach, FL: Health Communication, Inc., 2004), 69.

CHAPTER 8

Page 119 "Do one thing" Eleanor Roosevelt as quoted in Marcy Bryan, *Scared Silly: Taking on Your Fears, Worries, and What-Ifs* (Cincinnati, Ohio: Standard Publishing, 2007), 210.

Page 122 "Pretty much everyone" Author interview with Andy Pierce, April 2, 2010.

Page 124 "Behind this high aspiration" Chris Argyris, "Teaching Smart People How to Learn," *The Harvard Business Review*, May–June 1991: 7.

Page 127 "Decide that you want it" See http://lifehacker.com /5934640/decide-that-you-want-it-more-than-you-are-afraid-of-it.

Page 131 "To recast larger problems" Karl Weick, "Small Wins: Redefining the Scale of Social Problems," *American Psychologist*, January 1984: 40.

Page 131 "Don't be afraid" John C. Maxwell, *Talent Is Never Enough: Discover the Choices That Will Take You Beyond Your Talent* (Nashville, TN: Thomas Nelson, 2007), 110.

Page 133 "There is only one" Paulo Coelho, *The Alchemist* (New York: HarperCollins, 1998), 149.

CHAPTER 9

Page 135 "Pride costs more" Thomas Jefferson, "A Decalogue of Canons for Observation in Practical Life," Letter to the infant Thomas Jefferson Smith (February 21, 1825), http://memory.loc .gov/master/mss/mtj/mtj1/054/1200/1268.jpg.

Page 138 "Remembering that" Steve Jobs, Stanford commencement address, June 15 2005, http://news.stanford.edu/news/2005/june15/jobs-061505.html.

Page 141 "When we experience pride" Hale Dwoskin, *The Sedona Method: Your Key to Lasting Happiness, Success, Peace and Emotional Well-Being* (Sedona, AZ: Sedona Press, 2007), 91.

Page 141 "Vulnerability is not weakness" http://www.ted.com/talks/brene_brown_listening_to_shame.html.

Page 142 "He who would accomplish" James Allen, *As a Man Thinketh* (Radford, VA: Wilder Publications, 2007), 33.

Page 142 "I'm a great believer" Thomas Jefferson as quoted by Bob Kelly, *Worth Repeating: More Than 5000 Classic and Contemporary Quotes* (Grand Rapids, MI: Kregel Publications, 2003), 372.

Page 146 "often did just the opposite" Jim Collins, *Good to Great: Why Some Companies Make the Leap . . . and Others Don't* (New York, NY: HarperCollins, 2001), 39.

Page 148 "[People with a scarcity mentality]" Stephen R. Covey, *The 7 Habits of Highly Effective People* (New York: Free Press, 1989, 2004), 219-220.

Page 149 "are resolved to do" Collins, *Good to Great,* 39.

Page 150 "it is both a valuable asset" David Marcum and Steven Smith, *Egonomics: What Makes Ego Our Greatest Asset (or Most Expensive Liability)* (New York: Fireside, 2008), 7–8.

Page 150 "left unchecked" Ibid., 9.

Page 150 "When ego abandons humility" Ibid., 11.

CHAPTER 10

Page 153 "My own behavior" St. Paul, as quoted in Susan J. Heck, *With the Master in the School of Tested Faith* (Mustang, OK: Tate Publishing, 2006), 245.

Page 155 "Some years back" George A. Akerlof, *Explorations in Pragmatic Economics: Selected Papers of George A. Akerlof and Coauthors* (New York: Oxford University Press,

2005), 211. See also http://www.newyorker.com/arts/critics
/books/2010/10/11/101011crbo_books_surowiecki.

Page 155 "did not have rational" George Akerlof, *The American
Economic Review*, 81, (May 1991), 4.

Page 156 "Most drug abusers" Akerlof, *Explorations in Pragmatic
Economics,* 214.

Page 157 "Ironically, when I forced myself" Mike Michalowicz, "Are
You a Workaholic? You're In Trouble . . . Productivity Sucks!"
The Toilet Paper Entrepreneur, n.d., http://www.toiletpaper
entrepreneur.com/managing-focus/are-you-a-workaholic-your-in
-trouble-productivity-sucks/.

Page 157 "In the end, workaholics" Jason Fried and David Heinemeier
Hansson, *Rework,* 26, Google e-book.

Page 157 "Procrastinators live" Joseph R. Ferrari, *AARP Still
Procrastinating: The No-Regrets Guide to Getting It Done* (New
Jersey: John Wiley & Sons, Inc, 2010), Digital Edition.

Page 158 "scores of studies based" Piers Steel, *The Procrastination
Equation: How to Stop Putting Things Off and Start Getting Stuff
Done* (New York: HarperCollins, 2010), 25.

Page 158 "Procrastination is like going" "Temptations that are close
at hand are difficult to resist. Addicts often relapse after returning from treatment facilities because drugs and alcohol become
easily available and daily habits reassert themselves. Or we
load up on bread in the restaurant before the meal is served.
Or we check our e-mail 10 times an hour instead of completing
a project." "We're Sorry This Is Late . . . We Really Meant to
Post It Sooner: Research Into Procrastination Shows Surprising
Findings," *Science Daily,* January 10, 2007, http://www.science
daily.com/releases/2007/01/070110090851.htm.

Page 158 "Procrastinators seldom do" John Perry, "Structured
Procrastination," n.d., http://www.structuredprocrastination.com;
http://chronicle.com/article/10-Ig-Nobels-Awarded-/129224/.

Page 159 "dictionary definitions" *Oxford English Reference Dictionary*, 1996.

Page 159 "Latin roots of the" Earnest Klein, *A Comprehensive Etymological Dictionary of the English Language* (New York: Elsevier, 1971).

Page 159 "studies of vocational" E. V. Hooft et al., "Bridging the Gap Between Intentions and Behavior: Implementation Intentions, Action Control, and Procrastination," *Journal of Vocational Behavior* 66 (2005): 238–56.

Page 159 "academic journals" Gregory Schraw et al., "Doing the Things We Do: A Grounded Theory of Academic Procrastination," *Journal of Educational Psychology* 99 (2007): 12.

Page 160 "When it is hard to" Bart Anthony Kamphorst, "Reducing Procrastination by Scaffolding the Formation of Implementation Intentions," Utrecht University, Graduate School of Humanities Department of Philosophy, (October 2011): 22.

Page 160 "My own behavior baffles" St. Paul, as quoted in Susan J. Heck, *With the Master in the School of Tested Faith* (Mustang, OK: Tate Publishing, 2006), 245.

Page 161 "Procrastination is the grave" Procrastinators Anonymous, n.d., http://procrastinators-anonymous.org/.

Page 162 "You must never find" Charles Buxton, as quoted in Rex Hickox, *Time: Friend Or Foe* (Bentonville, AR: Rex Publishing 2006), 122.

Page 163 "The ability to simplify" Hans Hoffman, as quoted in Craig L. Sanders, *Keys to Manifesting Your Destiny* (Fairfax, VA: Xulon Press, 2008), 43.

Page 163 "Things which matter" Johann Wolfgang von Goethe, as quoted in Brian Tracy, *Eat That Frog! 21 Great Ways to Stop Procrastinating and Get More Done in Less Time* (USA: ReadHowYouWant, 2008), 27.

Page 165 "S.M.A.R.T." G. T. Doran. "There's a S.M.A.R.T. Way to Write Management's Goals and Objectives," *Management Review* (AMA Forum) 70:11 (1981) 35–36.

Page 165 "Specific: Goals must" Paul J. Meyer, as quoted in "Mentor Resources: Goal Setting," The Association of Science and Engineering Technology Professionals of Alberta, n.d., http://aset.ab.ca/pages/Membership/MentorResources.aspx; http://en.wikipedia.org/wiki/SMART_criteria.

Page 167 "A lot of people write" Jordan Goldberg, as quoted in John Blackstone, "The Whys and Why-Nows of Procrastination," CBS News, February 22, 2010, http://www.cbsnews.com/2100–3445_162–6228451.html.

Page 169 "If you really want" James A. Owen, *Drawing Out the Dragons: A Meditation on Art, Destiny, and the Power of Choice* (Salt Lake City, UT: Shadow Mountain, 2013), 7.

CHAPTER 11

Page 171 "I want you to be" Confucius, as quoted in Dax Crum, *Relentless,* n.d., 117, Google e-book.

Page 173 "I would rather" Author interview with Mike Colón, June 20, 2012.

Page 174 "Whatever the risks" Ibid.

Page 175 "The secret is authenticity" Oprah Winfrey, as quoted in Ileane Rudolf, "Exclusive Q&A: Oprah Winfrey Celebrates 25 Years," *TV Guide,* August 24, 2010, http://www.tvguide.com/News/Exclusive-Oprah-Winfrey-1022142.aspx.

Page 176 "I want you to be everything" Confucius, as quoted in Dax Crum, *Relentless,* 117.

Page 178 "You cannot travel" James Allen, *As a Man Thinketh* (Radford, VA: Wilder Publications, 2007), 36.

Page 179 "Marissa Mayer was one" See http://www.forbes.com/profile/marissa-mayer/.

Page 179 "50 Most Powerful Women" "50 Most Powerful Women," CNN Money, October 16, 2008, http://money.cnn.com/galleries

/2008/fortune/0809/gallery.women_mostpowerful.fortune/50
.html.

Page 179 "When speaking at" http://www.youtube.com/watch?v=ja
KoMCujc2k&feature=player_embedded.

Page 179 "Doing something you aren't" "Marissa Mayer's IIT commencement address," May 16, 2009, YouTube video, http://www
.youtube.com/watch?v=jaKoMCujc2k&feature=player_embedded.

Page 181 "The Quiksilver in Memory" Justin Cote, "The 2011 Eddie
Invitees Announced," *Transworld Surf,* November 2, 2011, http://
surf.transworld.net/1000139977/news/the-2011-eddie-invitees
-announced/.

Page 181 "The Eddie" "A Ripple in the Ocean That Travels Around
the World," The Quiksilver in Memory of Eddie Aikau, November
2, 2011, http://quiksilverlive.com/eddieaikau/2013/

Page 181 "but those rare and special" Justin Cote, "The 2011 Eddie
Invitees Announced."

Page 181 "On January 21, 2011" "Final Touches Being Made
by Moonlight at Waimea Bay, Call to be Made at 6:30AM
Thursday," Association of Surfing Professionals, January 20,
2011, http://www.aspworldtour.com/2011/01/20/final-touches
-being-made-by-moonlight-at-waimea-bay-call-to-be-made
-at-630am-thursday/.

Page 182 "However, 'after 4 hours'" Dave Reardon, "Part of what
makes The Eddie go is The Eddie not going," *Star Advertiser,*
January 21, 2011, http://www.staradvertiser.com/sports/20110121
_Part_of_what_makes_The_Eddie_go_is_The_Eddie_not_going
.html.

Page 182 "The waves weren't 'big'" Ibid.

Page 182 "actually clapped" Ibid.

Page 182 "This event has created" See http://surf.transworld
.net/1000139977/news/the-2011-eddie-invitees-announced/.

Page 183 "The essence of being real" Stewart D. Friedman, *Total*

Leadership: Be a Better Leader, Have a Richer Life (Boston, Massachusetts: Harvard Business School Publishing, 2008), 29.

Page 184 "To believe something" Gandhi, as quoted in Stephen M. R. Covey, *The Speed of Trust: The One Thing That Changes Everything* (New York: Free Press, 2006), 69.

Page 184 "To paraphrase the words" Paul Boese as quoted in Larry Chang, *Wisdom for the Soul: Five Millennia of Prescriptions for Spiritual Healing* (Washington, DC: Gnosophia Publishers, 2006), 321.

Page 186 "Find your voice" Ibid.

Page 186 "[Authentic people are] actively" "The similarity among these perspectives, and many of the subsequent perspectives discussed in this section, is the portrayal of people in a manner that transcends measuring success primarily via hedonic qualities (e.g., happiness), or even basic evolutionary success (e.g., survival). What emerges in its place is a broad depiction of people as being rich in complexity, actively and intentionally pursuing a life in accord with their deepest potentials." Michael Kernis and Brian Goldman, "A Multicomponent Conceptualization of Authenticity: Theory and Research," n.d., 285.

Page 189 "In any field" Author interview with Jonathan Canlas, June 17, 2012.

CHAPTER 12

Page 193 "He drew a circle" Edwin Markham, *Foundation Stones of Success—Volume III* (Chicago, IL: The Howard-Severance Company, 1910), 177.

Page 195 "Only I had been" Mohandas Karamchand (Mahatma) Gandhi, *Autobiography: The Story of My Experiments with Truth*, translated by Mahadev H. Desai (Boston: Beacon Press Books, 1993).

Page 199 "would rather die" Ibid., 430.

Page 200 "Successful people are" Brian Tracy, as quoted in Wes

Williams and Tamara Hendricks-Williams, *Stick to Your Vision: How to Get Past the Hurdles & Haters to Get Where You Want to Be* (Plattsburgh, NY: McClelland & Stewart Ltd., 2010), 223.

Page 201 "Some believe his murder" Craig and Marc Kielburger, "Craig's Story: 'I'm Only One Boy,'" in *Me to We: Finding Meaning in a Material World* (New York: Fireside, 2006), 1.

Page 201 "was all about children" Craig Kielburger and Kevin Major, *Free the Children: A Young Man Fights Against Child Labor and Proves that Children Can Change The World* (New York: HarperCollins Publishers, Inc., 1999), 9.

Page 202 "So this is the issue" Ibid., 10.

Page 202 "Within no time" Craig and Marc Kielburger, "Craig's Story", 3–10.

Page 203 "Everybody can be great" Martin Luther King, Jr., "The Drum Major Instinct," February 4, 1968, http://www.theking center.org/archive/document/drum-major-instinct-ebenezer -baptist-church.

Page 203 "Kielburger, along with" http://www.freethechildren.com /about-us/our-story.

Page 203 "According to the Free" http://www.freethechildren.com /about-us/our-model.

Page 203 "Over 207,000 health kits" http://www.freethechildren .com/about-us/our-story/.

Page 204 "Oprah invited Craig" "Children Changing the World," *The Oprah Winfrey Show*, A Global Adventure: The O Ambassadors Launch, July 10, 2008, http://www.oprah.com/world/Oprah -and-Free-The-Children-Launch-O-Ambassadors; see also http://www.freethechildren.com/oambassadors/.

Page 204 "helper's high" Allan Luks & Peggy Payne, *The Healing Power of Doing Good: The Health and Spiritual Benefits of Helping Others* (Lincoln, NE: iUniverse.com, 2001), xiii.

Page 204 "You can't help someone" Norman Schwarzkopf, as quoted in John C. Maxwell, *The 21 Irrefutable Laws of Leadership*, 302.

Page 205 "The moment there is suspicion" Gandhi as quoted in Stephen M. R. Covey, *The Speed of Trust: The One Thing That Changes Everything* (New York: Free Press, 2006), 8.

Page 205 "It is literally true" Napoleon Hill, *The Law of Success, Volume III: The Principles of Self-Creation,* 65.

Page 206 "to do whatever it takes" Collins, *Good to Great,* 39.

Page 207 "Go: Start doing something" Author interview with Steve Hargadon, June 7, 2012.

Page 208 "Gratitude is not only" Cicero, as quoted in Michael A. Zigarelli, *Cultivating Christian Character* (Fairfax, VA: Xulon Press, 1984), 47.

Page 209 "A noble person is" Buddha, as quoted in Christopher Peterson and Martin E. P. Seligman, *Character Strengths and Virtues: A Handbook and Classification* (New York: Oxford University Press, 2004), 555.

Page 209 "Cultivate the habit" Wallace Delois Wattles, *The Science of Getting Rich* (Mineola, NY: Dover Publications, 2008), 36.

Page 209 "Of all the 'attitudes'" Zig Ziglar, as quoted in Ryan C. Lowe, "Say Thank You," in *Get Off Your Attitude: Change Your Attitude, Change Your Life* (Shippensburg, PA: Sound Wisdom, 2011), Google e-book, chap. 10.

Page 209 "When you are grateful" Anthony Robbins, as quoted in Lynn A. Robinson, *Real Prosperity: Using the Power of Intuition to Create Financial and Spiritual Abundance* (Kansas City, MO: Andrews McMeel Publishing, 2004), 153.

Page 211 "Silent gratitude" G. B. Stern, as quoted in Sara Hacala, *Saving Civility: 52 Ways to Tame Rude, Crude & Attitude for a Polite Planet* (Woodstock, VT: Skylight Path Publishing, 2011), 140.

Page 212 "In other words, certain" In Paolo Coletti and Thomas Aichne, *Mass Customization: An Exploration of European Characteristics* (New York: Springer, 2011), 2.

Page 213 "The sentiment which most" Adam Smith, *Theory of Moral Sentiments* (London: George Bell and Sons, 1875), 94.

Page 213 "Additionally, experts on positive psychology" M. E. McCullough et al., "The grateful disposition: A conceptual and empirical topography," *Journal of Personality and Social Psychology,* 82 (2002): 112–127.

Page 213 "Gratitude has the potential" Barbara Frederickson, as quoted in "Carolina in the News: Thursday April 8, 2010," The University of North Carolina at Chapel Hill, http://uncnews.unc.edu/content/view/3513/103/.

Page 214 "Asking is the beginning" Jim Rohn, as quoted in Michael E. Angier, Sarah Pond, Dawn Angier, *101 Best Ways To Get Ahead* (South Burlington, Vermont: Success Networks International, 2005), 31.

Page 219 "A man may fulfill" Oliver Wendell Holmes, as quoted in Judi Neal, *Edgewalkers: People and Organizations That Take Risks, Build Bridges and Break New Ground* (Westport, CT: Praeger Publishers, 2006), 68.

Page 222 "It all comes down" http://devingraham.blogspot.com/2012_05_01_archive.html.

Page 225 "A hundred times every day" Albert Einstein, *The World As I see It* (London: The Book Tree, 2007), 1.

Page 229 "I closed my eyes" "Chat transcript with Roger Staubach," Pro Football Hall of Fame, December 8, 2000, http://www.profootballhof.com/history/release.aspx?release_id=771.

Page 229 "When the ball came" Barry Horn, "Staubach, Pearson discuss genesis of 'Hail Mary' pass," *Dallas Morning News,* January 17, 2010, http://www.dallasnews.com/sports/dallas-cowboys/headlines/20100117-Staubach-Pearson-discuss-genesis-of-7095.ece.

Page 230 "And, when you want" Paulo Coelho, *The Alchemist* (New York: HarperCollins, 1993), 171.

Page 231 "The Cowboys certainly" "N.F.L. Wild-Card Playoffs:

1999 Cowboys Recall 1975 Super Bowl Team," *New York Times*, January 09, 2000, http://www.nytimes.com/2000/01/09/sports /nfl-wild-card-playoffs-1999-cowboys-recall-1975-super-bowl -team.html?pagewanted=all&src=pm.

Page 234 "Trust is the new" http://www.podcastingnews.com /content/2009/10/craig-newmark-on-the-future-of-new-trust-is -the-new-black/.

Page 234 "were so unhappy" D. Michael Abrashoff, "Retention Through Redemption," *Harvard Business Review* (February 2001): 1–7.

Page 236 "The *Benfold* is named" D. Michael Abrashoff, "Retention Through Redemption," *Harvard Business Review* (February 2001): 1–7.

Page 237 "Don't let the 5%" "Trust/Speed of Trust," Questions for Living, April 21, 2008, http://www.questionsforliving.com/categories /human-attributes/trust-speed-trust.

Page 238 "A high level of trust" Thomas L. Friedman, *The World Is Flat: A Brief History of the Twenty-First Century* (New York: Picador, 2007), 334.

Page 238 "A man who trusts nobody" Harold MacMillan, as quoted in James W. Komarnicki, *How to Teach Toward Character Development* (West Conshohocken, PA: Infinity Publishing, 2005), 95.

Page 238 "Build from trust" Richard Edelman and Neal Flieger, "The United States and the Trust Barometer," *The Washington Post,* January 5, 2011, http://voices.washingtonpost.com/davos -diary/2011/01/the_united_states_and_the_trus.html.

Page 239 "In times of constant change" Anthony Robbins, "How to Thrive in a Changing Business World," n.d., http://www.tony robbins.com/events/unleash-the-power-within/white-paper.php.

Page 239 "As soon as you trust" Johann Wolfgang von Goethe, as quoted in Terry Cole-Whitaker, *Live Your Bliss: Practices That*

Produce Happiness and Prosperity (Novato, CA: New World Library, 2009), 123.

Page 240 "Self-trust is the first" Ralph Waldo Emerson, as quoted in Maureen Healy, "Shaping Self-Trust: Is Self-Trust Teachable?" *Psychology Today,* January 5, 2009, http://www.psychologytoday.com/experts/maureen-healy.

Page 241 "The best way to find" Ernest Hemingway, as quoted in Andrew Thompson, *The Hemingway Solution* (Bloomington, IN: AuthorHouse, 2009), 79.

Page 242 "The more isolated" Edward M. Hallowell, "Overloaded Circuits: Why Smart People Underperform," *Harvard Business Review* (2005): 4.

Page 243 "You don't have to be" Joe Sabah. See http://www.joesabah.com

CHAPTER 13

Page 245 "Give me a place" Archimedes, as quoted by Pappus of Alexandria, *Collection* or *Synagoge,* Book VIII, c. A.D. 340; Greek text: *Pappi Alexandrini Collectionis,* edited by Friedrich Otto Hultsch (Berlin, 1878), 1060. See also http://www.math.nyu.edu/~crorres/Archimedes/Lever/LeverIntro.html.

Page 252 "Individually, we are" See http://www.ryunosukesatoro.org/.

Page 256 "Weak ties" Linda Hill and Kent Lineback, *Being the Boss: The 3 Imperatives for Becoming a Great Leader* (Boston: Harvard Business School Publishing, 2011), 110.

Page 259 "Jobs landed a summer job" See http://www.hp.com/retiree/history/founders/hewlett/quotes.html.

Page 260 "That's how I'm going" See http://thenextweb.com/apple/2011/10/22/steve-jobs-helped-googles-page-facebooks-zuckerberg-to-repay-silicon-valley/.

Page 260 "Half of the world's" See http://www.un.org/summit/poverty.html.

Page 263 "Nobody does anything great" John C. Maxwell, *21 Irrefutable Laws of Leadership* (Nashville, TN: Thomas Nelson, 2007), 111–17.

Page 263 "display excellence" Ibid., 135.

Page 264 "There are so many" Alan M. Webber, *Rules of Thumb: 52 Truths for Winning At Business Without Losing Yourself* (New York: HarperCollins, 2009), 191.

Page 265 "We feel what we" Mother Teresa, *A Simple Path*, compiled by Lucinda Vardey (New York: Random House, 1995), 115.

CHAPTER 14

Page 267 "Never give up" See http://www.positivelypositive.com /quotes/never-give-up-on-something-that-you-cant-go-a-day -without-thinking-about/.

Index